READY SET GROW!

DEVOTIONS FOR TEENS

Kyle Dodd

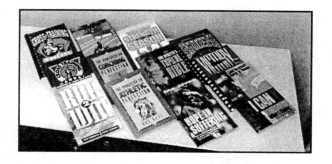

For additional books and resources
available through Cross Training
Publishing contact us at:
Cross Training Publishing
P.O. Box 1541
Grand Island, NE 68802
(308) 384-5762

READY, SET, GROW!

Library of Congress Cataloging-in-Publication Data

Dodd, Kyle
Kyle Dodd

Ready, Set, Grow! / Kyle Dodd
Published by Cross Training Publishing, Grand Island, Nebraska
68803

Distributed in the United States and Canada by Cross Training
Publishing

Cover Illustrator: Jeff Sharpton
Printed in the United States of America

INTRODUCTION

I once heard Dr. Howard Hendricks of Dallas Theological Seminary say during one of his classes, "If you're gonna' bore people...don't bore them with the Bible." The purpose of this book is two-fold: First, to take a gold nugget of Scripture written 2,000 years ago and inject into our modern day agendas, through the help of illustration, personal stories, and word pictures. Secondly, to be used as a tool for carving the truth into our hearts by the Master Craftsman.

Here is a fun side note...as a purchaser of this book you have donated the proceeds to sending an inner-city youth to Kids' Across America, A Christian Sports Camp, targeted at helping inner-city kids find hope through Christ. My prayer is that you learn as much about your Savior by reading it as I did writing it!

I'd like to take a moment of your time to give credit where credit is past due. First to my Father in Heaven who gave me the vision, to my wonderful family for encouraging me to seek the vision, to Janee,' Darnell, and the rest of the Kanakuk Kamp family who helped make the vision an object, and lastly to my lifetime accountability partners Joe, Coopie, and Bruce, for holding me to a standard I can't hold myself...Thanks!

Kyle Dodd

FOREWORD

The first time I met Kyle Dodd was during the summer of 1993 at Kanakuk Kamp. He reminded me of a military officer—the well thought-out disciplined, determined type. While at Kamp (Kanakuk) I went to a meeting where Kyle was the speaker. It was encouraging for me to find someone that spoke the truth in love, especially in a society where it is more socially acceptable to skirt the issues and live as through there are no absolutes. Kyle is more interested in challenging the youth in America than he is in gaining their approval, and as a result, God has truly blessed him and his ministry.

If you're like me, a life of devotion sometimes becomes an exercise in keeping score, rather than an opportunity for growth. This book will meet you exactly where you are and will challenge you to a deeper level of commitment through a series of practical devotions. These devotions are based on the Word of God, Kyle's life experiences, and other interesting angles that bring the Word of God alive. In a world where youth are searching for the truth, Kyle is a man that is giving them an opportunity to find just that...The Truth.

Michael Tait
of DC TALK

THE LAST WORD

"I am a little pencil in the hand of a writing God who is sending a love letter to the world." Mother Teresa

Who has the last word? No doubt about it, God definitely has the last word! But, all of Kyle's friends (I'm so fortunate to be one of those) will tell you that Kyle has the next to the last word. He's fun, he's loony, he's creative, he's animated, he's easier'n a puppy to fall in love with, he talks a million miles a minute, but best of all, he has a raging heart for kids of all ages. Nothing makes him more excited than seeing young folks become ingrained in God's word and committed to the Savior who wrote it. Folks, one experience in this devotional book each day will put jet fuel in your spiritual pipes and fuel your fire with enthusiasm for the Creator of the paper it's written on.

Please heed this warning as you turn the page...if you should dare to read one of these devotions each day and commit your life to the truth shared, you had better prepare yourself for some drastic changes in your life. You're probably going to like what you see in the mirror a whole lot more, your face is probably going to smile a lot more than people around you are used to, and a surge of God's grace, peace, and forgiveness may just invade your soul for a lifetime. As Walt Disney said, "Get a good idea and stay with it. Dog it, and work at it until it's done, and done right." Reading this book daily is one of the best ideas that's come along in years.

Joe White, Ed. D

A Bird's Eye View

READY, "*Those who wait on the Lord will gain new strength; They will mount up with wings like eagles. They will run and not get tired, they will walk and not become weary.*" *Isaiah 40:31*

SET, Every year in Branson nestled down in the colorful Ozark mountains about the time the tourists begin to depart and the snows begin to fall, we have a visitor arrive. No, it's not a long time friend stopping by for a hot meal, or a neighbor coming by for a cup of sugar, but a beautiful picture of our American heritage in flight. If you haven't guessed it by now, you'll do no good on the TV show *Jeopardy*...it's a bald eagle. For the past ten years, and I'm sure it went on long before I moved here (being creatures of habit), this eagle has come from a summer home up north, to stake his claim on giant tree tops down by the lake. What an awesome sight to see this eagle soaring to incredible heights looking for a meal by water or land. What a perspective of this world a bird of this magnitude must have on his surroundings and circumstances.

Do you ever wish that you could just mount up on a set of super-sonic wings and take off? Do you wish you could escape all problems and pains and get up above them all for some relief? Believe it or not, that's exactly why the prophet Isaiah tells us to mount up on these wings, so that we can gain a new perspective on life. Realize that at times you can't see the trees because of the forest, when you are in the midst of the trial. With God as our wings we soar out of the forest of pain, problems, sorrow, etc., we can get up, up and away (sounds like Superman) from them, and put life into perspective. Sometimes things aren't as tough with a vantage point. Sometimes pain isn't as bad with the right viewing advantage. You and I as Christians in America today need to get another view (God's view) on our circumstances to help us see why God is allowing us to encounter this challenge. So, the next time your problem seems too big to handle, here is some advice...mount up and take off!

GROW! What do my problems look like from another perspective? Why?

LET GO AND LET GOD

READY, *"She came to Him and began to bow down before Him, saying 'Lord help me!'" Matthew 15:25*

SET, You've heard the phrase 'let go and let God' for years. I never really understood that principle until the summer of 1970, on a small island in the middle of Lake Texoma where some friends and I would go hang out during the summer. I was only twelve at the time and about as smart as a box of rocks. My three friends, Bobby, Jeff, Billy, and I were doing our best to recreate an old war movie we saw the night before. I remember a large mound of sand that must have piled up from high water which we decided would be great to tunnel through to make a series of connecting fox holes. My buddies were gathering some tree limbs while I, the macho nacho, was digging this termite tunnel. As you have probably figured out by now, sand is the worst to try to dig in, because it has no strength to hold up walls. The tunnel collapsed on me, so all that was left showing was my Chuck Taylor basketball shoes. Immediately my vision became blackness and the oxygen became non-existent. I'm sorry to say I lost it and panicked. I began to kick, scream, twist and turn like a wind up toy gone mad. My friends returned to find me trapped and tried to grab my feet and pull me out backwards. There was only one small problem...they couldn't catch my feet, because I was kicking like an Olympic swimmer. Finally, after I had used all the air left in that pocket, I passed out. At which time, my friends could free me from the hole.

How many times in our lives do we kick, twist, rant and rave in a situation before we finally let go and let God? God seems to always be there at the right time, but we seem to think we wear an 'S' on our chest and can 'get out of this ourselves.' Why is it that there are always two ways to do things, our way and the right way? Allow God to take control of your life in chaos without kicking him away. All He wants to do is help us out of our holes, and all we need to do is relax and let Him. Take it from an ex- fox hole digger...it sure is good to see the light at the end of the tunnel.

GROW! What holes have you dug yourself into lately? Are you kicking God or allowing Him to free you? Why or why not?

THE REAL THING

READY, *"Jesus Christ is the same yesterday and today, yes, forever."*
Hebrews 13:8

SET, When was the last time you were at your local Quik-Trip store and asked the attendant at the register for a Coke? You were probably presented, after the strange, clueless look, with a barrage of selections like nothing you've ever seen with the naked eye. You can get a Classic Coke, New Coke, Coke in a bottle, in a can, in a plastic bottle or liter, diet, sugar free, caffeine free, diet caffeine free, cherry...need I go on? Why does it take an act of Congress to make a decision that used to be a no brainer? It seems we have taken everything fun out of the 'real thing' and made it into a close twin of pond water.

Isn't it a relief to know that our God is not watered down and changing as Coke is? What a nightmare just to think that Jesus would not be consistent in our future. What if He, just one day, woke up on the wrong side of a cloud in a bad mood and decided you weren't welcome in His family anymore? What if He decided we were saved by our works not grace, so we had to earn our way to those pearly gates? What if...He decided He didn't love you and was tired of playing with what He created and dumped you like a hot potato? There is comfort in knowing that the Original is still the Original; the Classic is still the Classic, without any of the vital ingredients removed for the sake of keeping up with the fads of society. Read it again (I'll wait)......................" Jesus is the same forever and ever." Amen (Look out Randy Travis). This translates into having a Savior who follows through with what He started in perfecting us daily. Now, sit back, relax, and ponder this some time today, and do yourself a favor, treat yourself to the 'Real Thing.'

GROW! What would it be like if Jesus wasn't the same today as He was two thousand years ago? How does consistency make you feel?

4

CASH MONEY

READY, "For the love of money is the root of all kinds of sin; some have wandered from the faith and pierced themselves with many griefs." 1 Timothy 6:10*

SET, You can't live with it and you can't live without it. What is it? Cold, hard, cash money. There is nothing more consistently found in society today that causes marriages to malfunction, companies to crumble, and societies to become stale, than money. I heard recently of an individual friend of mine who for the love of money lost a thriving business, his loving wife, and now his blue-eyed, blonde-haired children. I spoke with this person on the phone and asked him a direct question, "Was it worth it?" You don't have to be a rocket scientist to figure out his answer... "No, no, no!" You can look throughout history and see that the dynamite that destroys so many circumstances is what is produced by the Department of Treasury daily. Guess what though? It's not the money itself that is the problem...it's the *love of it.* It's kind of like that cute toy poodle at your grandparents house that looks harmless yet will bite the fire out of ya' when you touch it. Money can be a good thing if it's managed from a Godly bank account. You can probably name several people (not many) that have lots of money yet keep it all in perspective. You'll probably also notice that those people who play with the poodle and don't get bitten are believers and givers.

Realize this, that money is the root of all types of evil if it's loved, and God gives and God takes away at His own free will. Don't get swindled by the theory that waits out there for you right after college graduation that tells you that 'to have is happiness.' That's one piece of advice that's not worth its weight in gold.

GROW! How does the love of money affect you? How can you begin to de-program yourself of the thinking that money buys happiness?

READY, *"But if you show favoritism, you are committing sin and are convicted by the law as transgressors." James 2:10*

SET, A couple of snow-to-snows ago (that's American Indian talk for 'years'), I had the opportunity to see the President of the United States, George Bush, when he came for a campaign speech at a local theme park. Talk about an event of the century! Talk about rolling out the red carpet for someone! Oh my! I could not believe what a big to-do it was just for a guy to talk to a few thousand folks. Streets were blocked off for miles, Secret Service agents swarmed like bees, and a fleet of limos cruised in, and presidential helicopters filled the airways like a flock of geese. Come on, I mean how many folks does it take to protect one guy; and how can the President fly in all those copters at once? (Split personality, maybe?) I was amazed at how people from all around the community basically laid down everything to be of service to a guy who would make a speech, then jet set off to four other cities to repeat this brouhaha again.

We seem to live in a world that will only roll out the red carpet to those that are in high places. We idolize politicians, doctors, lawyers, movie stars, and athletes, but little do you see someone ask the grocery store bagger for an autograph. The reason, a lot of times, that we play favorites is in hopes we will get a perk, a bonus, a break, a loan, a status quo from our efforts. God doesn't show favorites in who He loves and who He doesn't, does He? Can you imagine a Savior that would only die for those who would pay Him back later? Our light shines brighter when we treat everyone the same—the class clown, or the super star. It's not hard to treat the gifted with special effort, but how about those who aren't the socially accepted types? Then you need God's help. Come on, take a gamble and treat the peons like a president.

GROW! Find someone who'd never expect it, and roll out the red carpet for them today. How does it feel to love the unloved?

READY, *"Now we know what the law says, it speaks to those under the law, that every mouth may be closed and the world may be held accountable to God." Romans 3:19*

SET, This word will not come up in casual conversation at dinner. It won't appear on the prime time nightly news. It's not a category on the popular game show *Jeopardy.* You'll have to run with a different pack of folks to even use this word, yet it's essential to the survival of a concrete Christian today. What is this word? *Accountability.* The old dictionary defines it as "liable to be called to account for your action(s); responsible; capable of being explained."

About three years ago I realized at a ripe age of thirty two, how weak I was alone in my walk with Christ (I learn quick, don't I?). The older I get, the less confidence I seem to have in myself for fighting this battle called faith, alone. Late one night I was watching one of those educational television shows on the *Discovery* channel, and I saw how packs of wolves would patiently wait until their prey, a thousand pound caribou crossing the frozen terrain of northern Canada, would file off alone. It was at that moment, like the wolves knew they were on camera, that they would charge the victim, like bugs to a light and take it down suddenly, without remorse. What a scene to show on the tube (I bet the animal rights folks were ticked). How sudden, how pre-planned, what violence, yet how true even in our own lives. Satan is the wolf (dressed in disguise) who waits for us to single ourselves away from the fellowship of other believers in the herd and bites to kill. Accountability keeps us out of the jaws of consumption and into the fearless hands of our Father in Heaven. We are first called to be held accountable to God then to our agape friends *daily.* Accountability means having someone ask you the tough questions which matter in our walk with Christ. We need someone to not let us slack off and hold us to a standard we can't always hold ourselves to. Try it...I promise it's better than being prey in the jaws of sin.

GROW! Who can hold you accountable today? How will you be consistent? When will you start?

READY, *"Furthermore, you shall select out of all the people able men who fear God, men of truth, those who hate dishonest gain and you shall delegate to them and place them as leaders over thousands, hundreds, fifties and tens. So it will be easier for you, and they will bear the burden with you. If you do these things and God so commands you, then you will be able to endure." Exodus 18:21-23*

SET, Working with people, which all of us are doing or will be doing, is a fun task. One lost art that I see missing from the center-piece of the Godly living room is delegation. Webster's defines it as "to commit or entrust authority to another person as an agent." We have far too many people who need to do it all, all the time. The word 'training' (teaching) comes to mind here for the simple reason that those folks who have the philosophy 'if you want something done right, do it yourself' seem to have lost sight. Granted, you want your trainee (pupil) to fall on their face, but not lose face in a project. You see, Jesus used another word for training and that is discipleship.

In this passage, Moses takes a little advice from his father-in-law. Moses is to answer all questions, meet everyone's needs, and play referee too? Not alone, he's not. This is the scene where the pop-in-law flies onto the set and sheds a little wisdom of prior knowledge to the formula of leadership/delegation (they go hand-in-hand, you know). The formula for successful delegation of a project, or task, is to find folks who possess the character qualities listed in scripture, create the vision for them, then ask the 'delegate to be' to tell you what you told him before setting out on this voyage. First, make sure you don't set someone up for failure by delegating to him a task that you know he doesn't have the skills to pull off. You must know your people, as Jesus did. Second, the proper steps to training are as follows...number one, model how you want it done; number two, do it with the trainee; and number three, leave and let them do it alone. It's as simple as one, two, three. Try it!

GROW! What was the last thing you delegated? Did they qualify with the formula?

OLD MACDONALD HAD A...WAY?

READY, *"Now to him (Jesus) who is able to do immeasurably more than all we ask or imagine, according to His power that is at work within us." Ephesians. 3:20*

SET, As a parent, you will know that there is only one place to pull over on a cross country trip for lunch and that's.....the 'Golden Arches.' Yep, you guessed it—Mickey D's; Mac attacks; two all beef patties; hamburger heaven, and I'm sure you have more to add. I cannot believe how this burger joint attracts youth world-wide with the power of a magnet. You can't drive more than ten miles before seeing 'the sign' and the kids in your car go ballistic for a Big Mac or a Happy Meal. Kids of all ages seem to see right past other burger barns (you know how they all seem to clump together like a covey of quail) to see McDonald's. What kind of marketing monster do they have to create this mystique? Why do kids stampede over one another to get chicken nuggets and the toy at the bottom of the Happy Meal box?

Can you imagine what our local newspapers and TV news stations would be saying if we, as Christians, were as excited about the Bible as kids are about a Big Mac!? What if the kids were crawling over the seats as fast for church as for chicken nuggets? What if we didn't need a Happy Meal to make us happy?! Guess what? We don't! We have Jesus! That's right, we can actually get excited about a Savior that does more for us mentally, physically and spiritually daily than any McLean could think about. Come on, let's start showing this dark world we live in what Christians on fire for their God look like. But, as you know, excitement burns calories, so you may want to take a detour to you-know-where, for some fuel for your fire.

GROW! What would it take for you to really get excited about what Jesus is doing for you right now and share it with someone? Just do it!

READY, "Men who understood the times with knowledge of what they should do." 1 Chronicles 12:32

SET, What if you went into a final exam without studying or challenged a team without scouting them first? We live in an information rich country which prides itself on being there when the action happens. News stations and major networks spend millions of dollars on equipment designed to allow live broadcasts from random locations. If you want to find out what has happened in our world, country, or cities in the last ten minutes, all you need is a remote or twenty-five cents for a paper. We have the capability (or technology) to be on top of the trends and times in a matter of minutes. The warning is that we can be fed the wrong perspective on the wrong story. In other words, our madness of media is a melting pot for a secular humanistic view. Our liberal media can spoon feed us, from behind the desk of the nightly news, a method of thinking and viewing certain situations. We, as a nation, saw the power of the media during the presidential race between George Bush and Bill Clinton.

You have a responsibility and a duty to keep up with what's going on around you. I like to say, "keeping your finger on the pulse of the times." You can do this by watching the news, reading the papers, listening to tapes, and reading books. Make sure these sources are reliable and conservative in nature. Don't just say this world is going downhill fast without making an effort to re-direct its course to the Cross. We, as Christians, are not of the world, yet we do live in the world by Divine design. Understanding the times of our world will help you direct your life. View the news with a critical eye and acknowledge it's run mostly by secular people who have not the knowledge of Christ. Make sure you spend more time studying the original (Bible) and not the counterfeit. Doing this allows you to tell what is true and what is false.

GROW! How much do you understand the times in which we live? How can you prevent being fed slanted liberal news? What one area will you choose to do something about?

READY, *"Let no one be found among you who practices divination or sorcery, interprets omens, engages in witchcraft or one who casts spells, or who is a medium, or spiritist, or who consults the dead. Anyone who does these things is detestable to the Lord." Deuteronomy 18:9-12*

SET, I heard a saying one time that said, "If you don't know where you're going, you'll probably get there." Our world is falling all over itself with people going nowhere. Daily you can read about someone on this planet that tries his hand at being or coming up with a new way of doing things. The *New Age Movement* is a rapidly growing cult of followers that at first glance seem to have the winning ticket for happiness. Words that spill from their mouths are words like psychic, Nirvana, astrology, self-realization, reincarnation, pantheism, out-of-body experiences, transformation, channeling, ESP, karma, and Shirley McClain. They practice their religion with tools such as crystals, yoga, ESP, Ouigi boards, and tarot cards. The reason this cult has taken off like a bullet out of a barrel is it requires no sacrifice at all, and it's a tremendous self-image builder. Their doctrine is 'If everything is god, then *I* am god.'

The movement is all about no higher moral absolutes and that truth is perceived individually. The New Age Movement derides the biblical doctrine of sin and substitutes reincarnation as the means of atonement. They believe there is no reality; therefore, all deaths lead to another life on earth in another form (who knows, maybe you'll return as a cockroach).

Realize that this is one of many types of cults in today's world, and they all are dangerous to tangle with. You'll see where Christians have retreated in society (i.e. Hollywood, politics, music, etc.) as this movement has advanced. The goal of new agers is to change 'how I feel' (it's all a feeling). How can we help in throwing a wrench in its gears? First, pray. Then, be a light in a dark world. Love your enemy. And finally, wear your armor daily (time in the Word).

GROW! Have you been approached or seen this movement in your community? How can you better prepare yourself today for this battle?

A Friend In Deed

READY, "A man (or woman) of many friends comes to ruin, but there is a friend who sticks closer than any brother." Proverbs 18:24

SET, You can't live with 'em, and you can't live without 'em. If there is one area considered as important as tick spray is to a dog, it's *friendships.* Every person alive today (including you) desires close, intimate relationships with others outside of dating. The one thing all these high-powered psychologists and psychiatrists, both secular and Christian, agree upon, is that everyone has two desires. One is the need to be loved the second is the need to love someone else. You know our dating relationships would be a lot longer lasting and closer if they started out as a friendship first and then graduated into a dating relationship. Marriages would be easier and more fruitful if they were an extended friendship which blossomed into a lifelong commitment.

Growing up, I didn't come from a church-going, meal praying family. I attribute my spiritual guidance to my uncompromising Christian friends. The Bible says, "bad company (not the rock group either) corrupts good morals." How often we run around with whom we may call friends, but who are only mere acquaintances, in actuality. If we use God's definition of true friendship to pick our friends, I think we would not be as apt to say, "I have tons of friends." A real friend is one who is like-minded with you in beliefs, ethics, morals and standards, one who challenges you to grow closer with Christ before growing closer to him, one who will stick with you through the highs and lows, ins and outs.

God gives you the model relationship and then leaves it up to you to follow the instruction manual (Bible) and build it. Don't hang out with the pigs if you don't want to end up in the mud. If you have a friend (not acquaintance) who sticks with you like a fly to fly paper, then invest your heart in them. Use your tongue wisely and be as loyal as a dog is to his owner. Believe me, this will be one investment with big returns even when the market falls.

GROW! Who would you die for out of your friends today? Why or why not? Are the reasons derived from scripture?

READY, *"And God made man in His own image, in the image of God He created him, male and female He created them." Genesis 1:27*

SET, The scene opens in a mythical, magical city called Agrabah; the story opens with a peasant boy named Aladdin and his side-kick monkey Abu. Aladdin falls head over heels in love with a princess Jasmine but they are limited by law that she can only marry a royal suitor. Aladdin's life takes a turn when he finds a magic lamp that contains a fun-loving, wish-giving genie who turns this peasant into a prince. Something begins to smell up the room when an evil sorcerer named Jafar and his mouth-all-mighty parrot, Lago, want this lamp for their own devices. If Aladdin is to have victory in this battle and win the lovely lady's heart, he must learn to be himself...one rub of the lamp (wish) the Genie cannot grant.

People every day of their lives get up, look in a mirror and see the reflection of someone they don't feel will be accepted in society. They desire to soar on a magic carpet ride of fantasy into being someone they are not. How frustrating it is to have to decide daily who and what a person wants to be in view of an audience of critics. You might recall that the lovely princess ends up loving Aladdin for being himself, not the painted up phony prince. You too can be accepted by just being you. As they say 'U.B.U.' and that is enough for anyone to step back and admire like a Picasso painting. Don't forget that your mold was broken upon your delivery and that you will be the best 'you' that will ever be. Get this, you won't have to act a different way because, now you're acting naturally...the way God intended. Yes, the reality is that some will find fault in you no matter what, but you can enjoy the phenomenal fun of being whom God intended you to be since the beginning of time...anytime you wish! (Get it?)

GROW! Do you try to act like someone you're not? Whom, if you could, would you like to be like? Why? How valuable are you to God? Why? What comfort is there knowing you are unique in this world?

READY, *"For God sees not as man sees, for man looks at the outward appearance, but the Lord looks at the heart." 1 Samuel 16:7*

SET, Thank God we live by the laws of the Creator and not the created! It seems like we live in a world of public displays, or like fish in a fish bowl, where everything and everyone, is judged on appearance. This cosmetic cosmos we call earth seems to have lost its perspective on what really matters and what doesn't. I heard a story of a unique burglary which took place in the windy city of Chicago, but the robbers didn't steal anything. They broke into a department store and switched price tags to make cheap items expensive and expensive merchandise cheap. A few hours past the store's opening, one chilly Monday morning, the salespeople began to notice something was definitely amiss. It seems that Satan (the thief) has come into our store (life) and switched around our priorities. He has taken the superficial and made it more important than the inward qualities of the heart. Can you imagine marrying someone for their appearance only, knowing full well that we all get older, grayer, more wrinkled, and less mobile by the day? Whereas, our hearts (Jesus' temple) get better by the day and more attractive by the hour. How refreshing it would be to have someone walk up and say, "you have a beautiful heart," or "your heart gets better lookin' everyday!"

It never fails that God's way is the right way. What a difference it would make in our social system if we would see as God sees.

GROW! How do you feel today about yourself? Are you looking from God's eyes?

THE MEASURE OF A MAN

READY, "Consider it pure joy when you encounter various trials, knowing that the testing of your faith produces endurance." James 1:2-3

SET, I read a quote once that said "A tree is best measured when it's down." All of my life, one of the things I looked forward to the most was cutting down big, tall, dead trees for firewood. Nothing makes you feel more manly than getting out the ol' Stihl chain saw and going to town on a tree that would make Paul Bunyon proud. Years ago, I was with a friend who was new (to say the least) to the sport of wood cutting. We had an okay from the Forestry Service to cut down and clear an area of National Forest, so we loaded up the trucks with chain saws and gas, and headed out for a hard day's work droppin' trees. My friend picked a tree far too big for a beginner to start on, which would prove to him that cutting down a tree is an art, not a game. He proceeded to cut around the trunk of this tree for the next hour to have it fall right on him and his saw, hard enough for him to see stars on a cloudy day. He later stated his surprise that the test for his tree cutting 'class' had been such a difficult trial.

God's word tells you that as a Christian your tests *will* come in all shapes and forms. We are told by Jesus' half-brother, that the trials and tough times of our lives are for the good of our faith, and the end product is the endurance to make it through more to come. You see, trials are a part of the curriculum of God's classroom, and you are to be joyful in knowing they are good for you and needed for strength. Just as my friend (who was fine after the stars faded out) learned that you can't really measure how you're doing until you're on the ground (in the midst of tough times), you too can see how deep your faith is, not when all is well, but when all seems to be wrong.

GROW! What trial faces you today? How can you handle it and be joyful?

READY, "For the time will come when they will not endure sound doctrine, but wanting to have their ears tickled, they will accumulate for themselves teachers in accordance to their own desires." 2 Timothy 4:3

SET, It was a Saturday night, and like most Americans who have a VCR, I decided to rent a movie and settle in by the fire for an entertaining evening at home. Our favorite movies are the clean but funny type, which are rare releases in the video stores today. This picture met all expectations and even ended with a good ethical ending. One line in the movie from the lead actor really started my wheels in motion. Even though it wasn't intended to be a biblical truth, it sure came off as such. He was telling a beautiful young actress a truth that is a reality, yet sadly. It went like this; "...tell anyone what they want to hear and you can sell them anything." Wow! Was that a one, two punch off the silver screen script, or what? Read it again, because it's worth its weight in gold. How true it is on this earth that people can be easily deceived when they are told exactly what they *want* to hear, not what they *need* to hear.

Hanging around our population of pedestrians, one continually sees the dangerous effects of having our ears 'tickled' with the untruths of worldliness. These lies are found in locker rooms, corporate headquarters, classrooms, in the papers, amidst the media, and even in some so-called churches. Isn't it funny (really sad though) that the apostle Paul warns a young man whom he tabs as one with a kindred spirit, that days will come of such nonsense? Just read the Bible at face value, and you'll notice that God doesn't mince words or pull punches. When He taught, He spoke the truth amongst those who had been told a lie. Realize those two funnels of flesh (ears) that hang on the sides of your head can't be opened and closed at will. *You* have to dictate by your location what goes in and out. *You* have to clue in that those ears are a direct line to your mind, which is the feeder to your livelihood, your heart. Be careful who and what you listen to. Don't be sold a lie in exchange for your soul.

GROW! What tickles your ears? How can you regulate what goes in your mind? What has the world lied about to you today?

HUMAN BEING OR HUMAN DOING

READY, *"The Lord God formed the man from the dust of the ground and breathed into his nostrils the breath of life and the man became a human being." Genesis 2:7*

SET, One of the greatest books of the Bible lies within the first several pages where God shows off His awesome power and creativity. When we read the book of beginnings, God seems to show us how all this began, plus a side show of details. When God created you He intended you to be in a relationship with Him from day one. There is a reason we were made human beings and not human doings. A human being what? In love with its Creator! Yep, you read it right, a human selling out his heart and soul to the Master mechanic of two-legged folks. Our greatest commandment that Moses brought back from the mountain is to "Love the Lord God with all your heart, soul and mind." It seems like in this day and time, we tend to think we can actually pay God off with cheap works (doings) to get us to, or keep us in, those golden gates called heaven.

We are a society saved by *grace*, not by works (Ephesians 2:5). The word grace means to stoop or bow. You cannot earn the right to go to heaven, just accept the ticket (salvation through Christ) and say 'thank you' for the cross of calvary. My dad is a horse rancher. For years I have watched him walk stooped-over across a pasture, never standing higher than the horse, right up to a new-born colt, who has never seen a human before, and begin to rub and pet this colt that doesn't run away. Why? Because my Dad humbly stoops (with grace) in order not to intimidate the baby colt by his size or stature.

Take this to the bank and deposit it. You are called *first* to love God and develop a relationship, then the fruits of faith will follow. Try being what you were created to do and that's 'be.'

GROW! How intimate is your relationship to the Creator? How can it be better?

17

READY, *"Be anxious (worry) for nothing, but in everything by prayer and supplication with thanksgiving let your requests be made known to God." Philippians 4:6*

SET, What do people worry most about?
>   People (family and friends)
>   Things (material goods)
>   Future (job, relationships, spouse)
>   Appearance (physical looks)
>   Image (view others have of you)
>   Death (life after)
>   Pain (physically or emotionally)

Boy, if there is one area we all deal with on a daily basis, it's worry. It seems as though this creature rears its ugly head at every opportunity. We all desire a life of comfort and security (just look at how well insurance companies do), yet we live in a world of people and change. The older you get the deeper and taller the problems seem to get. How in the world are you to fight this monster and win a few battles? Once again the Bible seems to come up with yet another simple solution.

The apostle Paul, a man who had a lot to worry about, tells us that the key to this buried treasure lies in prayer. We are not to worry about 'anything' (yes, it means what it says), but our thought is to be thankful that we have a God above who cares about us down to the smallest details of daily life (Matthew 6:25-27).

Let's face it, if our lives were all comfortable and unchanging, we would not only be bored stiff, but we wouldn't have any use for a Savior. When you face the monster of worry, punch him with prayer.

GROW! What really worries you today? How are you going to deal with it?

READY, *"Be angry, and yet do not sin; do not let the sun go down on your anger." Ephesians 4:26*

SET, Have you ever had any of the following thoughts before? It's a sin to get angry. Don't share your angry feelings with anyone. God doesn't understand anger. Hold all anger inside. The best way to deal with anger is to ignore it. Jesus never got angry. Anger is only an outward feeling. Anger shows spiritual immaturity. God doesn't forgive anger. Christians just don't get angry.

Well, if you chimed right in on this 'top ten' list, then listen up, because what you see is not necessarily what you get. In this day and time, it's easy to get ticked off when you've been done wrong, cut off by another car, butted in front of in the checkout line, called something you're not, feeling like you've been dealt a bad hand in the game of life. Jesus himself felt these same feelings and emotions two thousand years ago. The most common verse remembered tells how He turned over mega tables set up by tax collectors in His Father's temple. But what about Mark 3:5 or John 3:36? These recorded instances were true expressions of anger by our Savior, and when looked intently upon equate to a slow rising type of anger in which Jesus is displeased with the situation, but handles it like it should be handled, without violence or destruction. There are two types of anger (news to me) that are defined, one which is Christ-like, the other which is man-made. One is targeted at the disobedience and defiance of God's word, and the other contains jealousy and bitterness (Galatians).

You see, anger, handled as Jesus did, is not wrong if its pure motive is to correct and set back on the right path to Christ. The other is purely of the world and results in violence and uncontrolled outbursts that stem from desires of the flesh. Make it a point to check the reason behind your anger first, then deal with it directly in accordance to scripture *before the sun goes down that day.*

GROW! What ticks you off the most? Why?

PRUNING

READY, *"Those whom I love, I rebuke and discipline; be excited and therefore repent." Revelation 3:19*

SET, Growing up in an area with lots of trees, many of which planted themselves right smack in the middle of my front yard, was fun but exhausting. As you know, where trees abound, so do a multitude of leaves each fall. People visiting our home used to make this awful big deal about the beautiful fall foliage but foreshadowed raking and bagging to me. Every year, like a tradition, my father and I would recover out of storage the chain saw and go to pruning the monster pecan trees, all twenty-one of them. Talk about a task that seemed endless! It was almost like we were creating more of a mess than making an improvement. Consider the viewpoint of the tree also. Man, did I think that all that cutting and cracking would produce some awful pain (if trees do feel). My dad could make a thirty foot high massive tree look like a nub in just a matter of a few coarse cuts. Little did my feeble mind know that this whole process was for the benefit, not the harm of the trees' future growth. God too, periodically goes and gets His spiritual saw and begins to trim off areas in your life that don't look like or act like His Son Jesus. Once as I watched a woodcarver chisel on a block of wood, another observer asked him what he was making. "An Indian warrior," the woodcarver replied. "How do you know which parts to carve away?" the onlooker then asked. "Everything that doesn't look like an Indian," said the carver.

God's purpose in disciplining you is to make you better and not to kill or destroy you. Realize He only does this pruning because He loves you. Your parents only put parameters and rules around you because they care, not because they want to hurt you. God only wants you to succeed in this journey we call Christianity and one way is to prune off the dead or heavy branches which could eventually destroy the tree (you). Next time your God or your loving parents prune away on you, look past the momentary pain and see the benefits that will come...a person who looks more like Jesus.

GROW! How has God pruned you lately? Did you feel His love? How do your parents show they care?

Male Bonding

READY, *"I am distressed for you, my brother Jonathan; You have been pleasant to me. Your love to me was more wonderful than the love of a woman." 2 Samuel 1:26*

SET, Whatever you do, don't judge these sensitive adjectives by their cover. Do they look perverted, or how about twisted? These words came from David as he describes, as best a man knows how, the love he has for another brother. It's tough to say, much less hear this descriptive dialog in the midst of today's society. What you're seeing here is a lost art in our make-up of men. Men need men to stand by them in those fox hole times. I don't want you ladies to stop reading here, because you could learn something about the male species if you'll continue. Who knows, maybe someday you'll get married and realize that yes, they are one with you, but they still need male companionship. Men desire (most won't admit it) to have a relationship that is real, strong, unconditional, compelling, and long lasting. Deep down in the depths of man's soul is a longing to be a friend, someone to lock arms with, a 'bro' who will cover another's backside in tough tangos.

Most men really never experience what it means to yoke themselves with another man in a natural God-made way. Why? Several reasons...maybe it wasn't modeled by a father figure; maybe they fear rejection; how about not knowing what vulnerability really is; they could be too busy with business; or maybe it's an image thing. Whatever the lame reason is, it's wrong. God gave us the tender example of David and Jonathan to exemplify what 'male bonding' really looks like in biblical terms. One reason men are falling by the wayside in crooked business deals, or from behind the pulpit, is because they have no male accountability. Don't get me wrong now ladies, yes, you are a huge part of accountability, yet men sometimes need another 'like kind' with whom to identify. In a social system that doesn't seem to allow male companionship without perversion, it's time we learn the importance of male bonding.

GROW! How important is male bonding? Do you see much of it in today's world? How would a strong male accountability partner help you?

A Fashion Statement

READY, "*Likewise I want women to adorn (dress) themselves with proper clothing, modestly and discreetly.*" *1 Timothy 2:9*

GROW! Look no further than your local newsstand to see the latest 'styles' trickling down the fashion pipe of the world. *Vogue, Seventeen, GQ, Glamour, Self, Fashion & Design, Elle,* and of course, *Cosmopolitan* to name a few. Fashion in this world of ours changes as often as do weather patterns. One minute you're making a fashion 'statement' and the next you're frowned upon as being out-of-date. If I have this figured out, the way I see it is that if you just hang on to the same clothes for a few years, they'll come back in style (*i.e.* bell bottoms, neons, wide ties, etc.). Now don't get me wrong, there are some things that will never be out-to-lunch, but that's not the norm. Psychologists claim that there are several ways people show their inward desires in an outwardly expression. For example, what we desire can be seen in the sort of car you drive, hairstyle you sport, and clothes you wear. The only problem with this 'expression' is that it seems to be moving in the 'less is better' direction. The shorter the dress or shorts, the tighter the pants, the more high cut and revealing the swim-suit the better...for who?

I know about right now you have decided this whole devo is targeted at the female and yep, that's a good guess. Why? Because women are like a crock pot (heat up slowly), and men are like a microwave (heat up fast). In other words, men are turned on much easier than women by sight. So when they see a 'cute young thing' running around half clothed, they get aroused quickly, which in turn leads to lustful thoughts (Philippians 4:8). Please, I beg of you, from the knees of all men trying to seek God's ways on everything, watch what you wear and how you present yourself to men. I don't know of anything that can steal a man's heavenly perspective quicker than a worldly outfit. I'm not telling you to buy all your clothes at the local Thrift Store, but I am asking you to ask yourself one question before you step into your closet or throw down the credit card...how comfortable would you feel if Jesus stepped into the room while you were wearing what you had on? Make a fashion statement for Jesus...dress modestly.

GROW! Do you dress modestly or risky? How does this affect the opposite sex? What does Luke 17:2 mean?

READY, *"Arise, shine, for your light has come, and the glory of the Lord has risen upon you." Isaiah 60:1*

SET, For the first time in my life, at the age of thirty-five, I was convinced (by my wife) that I needed a taste of culture. One is never too sure if this 'taste' is gonna' be one that goes down easy or one that will pucker the lips like a dill pickle. My taste was a trip to the Big Apple (the city of a million hair-do's) to see a real, live Broadway show. Now you're never too sure which show is gonna' be the kind that will culture you or corrupt you. This particular show, *Crazy for You,* wound up being very entertaining and funny (expensive, too). The singers, dancers and theme were done tastefully with a mix of humor. Never in my wildest dreams did I see myself in New York City, dressed in a tie, watching a Broadway show and enjoying it (miracles still do happen).

The prophet Isaiah, thousands of years ago, spoke of a future cast of shining stars yet to enter their own stage called America. Even though the Broadway shows may disagree, there was a bigger show in town years before anyone ever thought up the *Will Roger's Follies* or *Annie.* The cast went like this: God was the Producer, Jesus was the lead actor, and the Holy Spirit was the director and they left *you* to sneak preview the show of the century. Let's think about this show for a moment. You and I are the previews of this Emmy award winning presentation to a world sitting in darkness.

First thing you have to get over is stage fright, then realize that it's not a show, it's a way of life. Don't think for one second you're not capable of being a star in this show. You were made to shine, so shine on!

GROW! What kind of preview are you presenting to your friends and family? How can you be a better star?

Excess Baggage

READY, *"For my iniquities have gone over my head; As a heavy burden they weigh too much for me." Psalm 38:4*

SET, It had been one of those days from the moment I got up at 7:00 a.m. I nearly melted my eyebrows with a hair dryer and my shirt had a giant grape juice stain on the back. I was scheduled to be in Denver by 1:00 p.m. for a connecting flight through Dallas/Ft. Worth Airport with a thirty-five minute lay-over. I opted not to check any bags below the plane for fear the airlines would pull a bonehead stunt and lose my luggage. My flight came in late to Dallas, not to mention that I almost had to use the barf-bag, and I was left with about ten minutes to catch the Denver plane 5 miles from the where we'd arrived. Okay, so I did my O.J. Simpson impersonation and ran down the terminal like a crazed halfback headed for the goal-line with four big bags flopping like crazy. Boy, did I nearly steam-roll about three children, two old people, a poodle, and a policeman (oops)! Needless to say, I missed my flight by about thirty steps, and on top of that, one of my bags broke open sending socks and underwear flying all over the terminal floor (how embarrassing).

As Christians we have times we carry excess baggage such as worry, anger, envy, jealousy, and bitterness while racing through the terminals of time. They become a heavy burden and at times too much to bear. Our knees buckle, our tempers go ballistic, and our attitude stinks, simply because we don't allow God to carry them for us. A lot of times people have adverse reactions like depression, violence, or even suicide as a release valve. Don't let your baggage encumber you to the point of wanting to quit. Cast your worries and all your troubles (bags) on Him because, He cares. Believe me, bags not only slow you down, they are a down right pain to deal with, and could cause you to miss your flight to happiness.

GROW! What bags are you carrying around with you through life? How can God help relieve you of the heavy burdens society weighs on you? Will you let him today?

SCAR FACE

READY, *"There is therefore no condemnation for those who are in Christ Jesus." Romans 8:1*

SET, If you've ever seen the move *Man Without A Face* staring Mel Gibson you know you left with an empty pit in your stomach at its conclusion. The setting of this movie takes place on the upper northeast coast with a dysfunctional family on summer vacation. The son (about twelve years old) has a desire to go to a military boarding school, but has been programmed by his family that he's not smart enough to pass the test to get in. The boy stumbles across a man (Mel Gibson) who has been burned badly over half his body who the locals call 'hamburger face.' This man, come to find out by the boy, is a previous teacher (now an artist) who ends up tutoring the boy for the entrance test. The small community isn't aware the boy has become such a loyal friend and is seeing the 'man without a face' regularly. Well, to make a long story longer, one evening after going on a hike, while driving back the boy looks over at the man's badly scared face and says, "You know, I can't even see your scars anymore."

Isn't it great that we (scar faces all) have a friend in Jesus who looks past all our faults to love us unconditionally? Isn't it reassuring to know that we live with a Creator who continues to tutor us and care for our daily need? You see, God is not real hung up on all this cosmetic community we dwell in as much as seeing our hearts with a need to know Jesus. You are so lucky (me too!) to be accompanied every second of our lives with a Spirit that will never leave of ditch us for something or someone better. Next time you feel sorry for someone for the way he was born or looks like (deformities and all), realize this, we all are like that yet through grace we were made special and unique. Next time you feel like 'Ol' Hamburger Face' realize God is in the business of making outcasts into works of art.

GROW! How often do you judge people pass or fail? Does God treat you like you treat others? How can you change your ways today?

READY, "*As Jesus approached the town gate, a dead person was being carried out, the only son of his mother, and she was a widow. And a large crowd from the town was with her. When Jesus saw her, his heart went out to her and he felt compassion and he said, 'Don't cry.'*" Luke 7:12-13

SET, On March 12, 1994 I received a phone call while in Telluride, Colorado, that won't quit ringing in my mind for a long time. The call was from my wife, to inform me of a very close friend of mine who had died of a heart attack in Houston, Texas. Wow...did this news stop me in my tracks. It was weird how I almost didn't seem to believe her (my own wife) and continued to interrogate her on the validity of the news. Death comes so quickly, yet it doesn't play favorites or give much warning of its arrival time. My purpose in this devo is not to set your day out on a down note, but to open your eyes to a grave reality. Throughout the entire funeral I noticed the joy on the some fifteen hundred faces attending. It was like those in attendance weren't as concerned with the loss of a friend as they were with the future of the hope. The tears came from loss of a friend, not from having to guess where he had gone. They knew ...heaven.

If you notice in the Bible, Jesus tells the mother of the deceased son not to cry. Why? Doesn't that seem a little harsh to stomach? After all, He had just stated that He felt compassion for her, right? I believe the reason for this statement by the Savior was because He was in total control. Have you ever noticed the ones who don't get tangled up in the turbulence of the times are those with a heavenly perspective? Remember, the vantage point which overlooks situations from above can be your's also. Now I'm not saying that crying is wrong and neither is God, as long as your heart realizes that Jesus cares for you and your situations and He holds the future. Hey, it's not bad having a Savior who exemplifies compassion and knowing my friend is residing with his Creator...what a set up!

GROW! If you were to lose a friend today how would you react? How does this scripture apply today?

READY, "*Purify yourselves for tomorrow the Lord will do wonders among you.*" *Joshua 3:5*

SET, The word purity seems to be used in the modern day language about as much as dinosaurs are used in a circus (let me give you a hint...never)! The thickest book in your library defines the word to mean "quality or state of being pure in thought and act." A pastor by the name of H.D. McCartney said it best, "The only power we have over our past is purity in the present."

Everywhere you look you see a corrupt world telling you purity is a thing of the past and your actions *today* will not affect you in the future. When you read the headlines, watch the tube, drive by the billboards, feast on the lyrics, and glance at the magazine covers, you will see a one sided report. Isn't it funny that God invented sex, to "be fruitful and multiply," before He allowed sin to exist? Isn't it ironic how we have taken a thing (sex) of beauty, designed to stay within the context of marriage, and allowed this deceiving world to turn the tables of creation? Your body is a beautiful temple designed to be a dwelling place of your Savior. Your desires are not evil, if handled by the hands of the Master Potter, spun for a specific time, place, and function.

As you sit here and chew on this nugget of scripture, allow commitment to enter through the doors of your heart. Make a deal with God on your knees that you will guard your heart, mind and body and wait 'til that special day when you will be the one on the alter looking into the loving eyes of the spouse you will share your life with 'til death do you part. It doesn't matter what you've done in the past, purity beginning today will do wonders among you.

GROW! What kind of commitment can you make today concerning your purity? Will you?

READY, "*The lamp of the body is the eye, if therefore your eye is clear, your whole body will be full of light.*" *Matthew 6:22*

SET, Talk about an outdoor experience! Little did I know, when I accepted an invitation to go on an elk hunting trip in a five million acre wilderness in Idaho, it would be such an adventure! Our trusty guide led us for five days over nine thousand foot mountain tops and through pine forests in search of the 'Big One.' The lessons about life in general and the parallels of my Christian life were as plentiful as mountain daisies in the springtime.

Our home was a tent, our water from a spring, our food...home cooked, and our transportation...horses and mules (look out wagon train!). Little did I know I would only get four to five hours of sleep a night and be on the back of a horse five hours a day. Each morning at 4:00 a.m. we would ride out of camp, straight up the mountains in pitch dark, on a twelve inch wide trail next to thousand foot cliffs where only the horse could see, searching for the bugle of a bull elk, relying solely on the eyes of our horse and guide. Never before have I depended on one of the five senses so heavily for my safety and my success in a hunt.

In one of the greatest sermons ever accounted, Jesus refers to the eye in a unique manner. Matthew 6:22 tells us that the "lamp of the body is the eye." The verse goes on to say "if your eye is clear, your whole body will be full of light." What worldly items clog our vision of God? What can you do at home to keep your eye clear? What does the lost society in which we live, see if we shine for Christ? Just as this thought hit me, during a ride on my horse 'Jock,' I realized how much we rely on our eyes (the hot-line to our hearts) to guide us toward our goal...not elk, but living for Christ. I understood how TV, movies, books and magazines can cause us to be spiritually blind, making us vulnerable as prey. Take a minute to look in a mirror at those beautiful eyes and see if the lamp is lit. If it's dim in there, do what it takes to get it shining brightly again.

GROW! Have you had an eye exam from the Savior lately? How's your light burning today?

READY, *"Finally, brethren, whatever is true, honorable, right, pure, lovely, of good repute, if there is any excellence and if anything worthy of praise, let your mind dwell on these things." Philippians 4:8*

SET, It's a pretty uncommon sight for a school, office, or now even a home to be without a computer. The *Age of Aquarius* has evolved into the age of technology. Schools are training our youth to use computers from kindergarten up. The computer has brought to the table organization, memory, data processing, and graphics like never before. You would think this conglomeration of wires, plastics, and micro chips had a mind of its own. Realize this, a computer is a tool, and only as smart as its programmer. *MicroSoft SuperPaint* and *ClarisWorks* weren't manufactured by a computer named Bob. Millions of dollars are being made by professional programmers coming up with and developing programs for business and personal computers. A computer takes the input, stores it, performs calculations or processes on it, then spit it back up as output when recalled (how's that for simplicity?).

Your mind is a *super computer.* When used properly, it is a tremendous tool that can recall details from years past, visualize scenes from TV shows and old movies, trigger emotions, control every muscle movement, distinguish between two means, and create new ideas. Whether you realize it or not, whatever you see and listen to (input), goes directly into your mind for processing. Every bed scene on TV, every curse word on the silver screen, every lyric at a concert, every word blurted out of the radio. You are being programmed by someone, and it's root is either in heaven or hell. Your mind is like a sponge, your eyes like a camera, catching every move and wiping up every worldly spill. Be *careful* and downright picky about what you watch, listen to, and who you follow. Set your mind on things above and not below. Be your own censor and screen the bad from your mind. Remember, what you are is connected to what you think.

GROW! How careful are you with your mind? Do you screen what goes in, or is it an open door policy?

We Are Overcomers

READY, *"He who overcomes, I will grant to him to sit down with Me on My Throne, as I also overcame and sat down with My Father on His Throne." Revelation 3:21*

SET, The popular soul Christian group called 'The Winans' had a song titled *We are Overcomers* in the early '90's. Listening to the words of that song (along with a great tune) made me realize just how blessed we are in life. To be a conqueror, one must first realize it's not an overnight ordeal, it's a process (t-i-m-e). Reflect back for a minute on all the great people of this world and I'll bet you a nickel they just didn't wake up one morning and arrive. Training is as important to our spiritual beings as it is to the sports stars. Isn't preparation a key to survival? We are done a great dysfunction, in one sense, through being programmed by society into thinking if it doesn't come quick then it's not worth waiting for. I call this the McDonald's Mentality. You know, when it takes the drive-through attendant longer than three minutes to get your order, you go ballistic and speed off.

I see a whole lot more preparation and persevering going on in scripture than I do quick fixes. Noah waited one hundred and twenty years; Sarah was ninety when she gave birth; Moses waited patiently; Paul walked miles on missionary journeys; Jonah lived in a whale belly, and Job went from something to nothing and back to something. Isn't it wonderful how we have a hero like Jesus who asked us to follow Him and do as He did? Look at that again, He wants you to overcome tough times. Why? Because He did first. Hey, I love playing follow the leader when my leader is worth following. God may call you to overcome sickness, a broken heart, the loss of a loved one, surviving with less 'things,' a personal setback in your career, or whatever. His promise is that when, not if, you overcome these challenges, you may sit with Him at the head of the table (the Throne). That's right...sit beside the One who holds every star in place. Now that promise from God is what I'd say is worth persevering for.

GROW! What trials have you overcome lately? How did God help you through? How can you prepare now?

Keeping It Clean

READY, *"Thy word have I treasured in my heart (and mind) that I may not sin against Thee." Psalms 119:11*

SET, A story is told of a family who lived in the deserts of Egypt. As the story begins, the family doesn't have all the modern conveniences, which we take for granted today, to make life easier. One day the father gave his young son a tightly knit reed basket and told him to go to the artesian well, about a mile away, fill up the basket with water and return home. The boy obeyed his father's request and set off across the hot desert sand in search of water. When he later returned home, to his surprise, all the water had leaked through the reeds, and all he had to show his father was an empty basket. To the sons confusion, the father instructed the boy to do the same the next day. After three trips across the hot tundra, the boy expressed frustration with his failure to deliver to his father. The father replied, "My son, the purpose was not to fetch water, but to clean the basket."

When Jesus was being tested in the wilderness by Satan himself, He used the tool of memorized scripture to fight His battles for Him. The armor of a Christian consists of only one weapon— the Word of God. The purpose of scripture memory is to purify (renew) our minds, but not necessarily to retain it. If you're like me, you may not be the most intelligent memorizer in the world. You've tried your hand at scripture memory, but two weeks later you've forgotten it completely. Yes, it is true, you won't keep what you don't use. But your labor is not in vain, because as you sit down and meditate on scripture, the Word is cleaning your mind of worldly impurities. In the rough, crowded world in which we live, we must do something other than sit in a recliner with a remote control. Memorizing the Word of God is tough, but worth every second of time you invest. Start tonight with a small bite (one verse) and quote it all day to yourself, and remember the journey is as fun as the final destination.

GROW! When was the last time you memorized a verse? What is the verse you're memorizing today?

READY, *"Therefore, since we have so great a cloud of witnesses sur-*
rounding us, let us also lay aside every encumbrance, and the sin which
so easily entangles us, and let us run with endurance the race that is set
before us." Hebrews. 12:1

SET, If you go to many track meets or cross country events, you
will find competitors who are basically made up of only two body
parts...legs and lungs. My hat is off to those courageous souls who
brave the weather and the big neighborhood dogs running loose, to
call themselves runners. America is full of pavement beaters who
rise up from slumber daily to get the old ticker (heart) in shape for
those later years of life. I, for one, standing six feet, five inches tall,
weighing in at two hundred twenty pounds and accompanied with
a flat size thirteen fleet of feet, am not one of that species. When I
run, it sounds like a wild herd of elephants escaping from the city
zoo and stampeding loose on the streets.

The Bible, over and over, uses the words *run* and *race*. The
Christian life is compared with a race and the Christian person
with a runner, who can enter as a participant because of Christ's
payment at the cross. The author of Hebrews tells us that in order
to succeed in this event, we need to throw off two things: every
encumbrance and the sin that trips us up. The sin, in this context,
is lack of faith; and the encumbrance is defined as excess weight. In
other words, to finish you need faith in God's way and prior training that will allow the weight of worldliness to be burned off like
calories.

How are you training today to be a competitive runner for
God? How deep is your faith in your Savior, that this race is the
most important race of your life? Do yourself a favor and get training for this one, because the reward you will receive beats the heck
out of any medal or trophy earned today.

GROW! What worldly weight are you carrying with you? How
can you lose it?

LET THE GAMES BEGIN!

READY, *"I give you this charge: Preach the word; be prepared in season and out of season; correct, rebuke and encourage with great patience and careful instruction." 2 Timothy 4:2*

SET, When September roles around and there is a cool, crisp, nip in the air, the smell of football season is a reality. Friday night football heroes begin to shine under the stadium lights like stars on a dark night. Where I grew up in Texas, the only thing that was worse than missing Sunday church was failing to make it to the hometown high school football game (and that was serious).

We seem to live our lives from season to season, waiting for the next sporting event to transpire. As an athlete competing in these events, you know the time, sacrifice and dedication it takes to pull off a victory on Friday night. Spectators only see a small percentage of what it takes to compete at a winning level and miss the months and hours of prior-to-season preparation training. Paul (the head coach), teaches his player (Timothy) a few lessons and game plans which he, through his years of experience as a competitor, learned about being a Christian player. The book of 2 Timothy is the last book that the apostle Paul wrote before his death. Can you imagine, as his pupil, how you would hang on every last word of wisdom? One of the last gold nuggets of truth given to Timothy was to train, not only in season, but also during the off season. Championships are won, not during season, but in the off season training in the weight rooms, on the track, and in the gyms after hours. Anyone can be motivated when there are people in the grandstands. Anyone can draw strength from within when the crowd roars with encouragement. But what about when there are no stands and no noise? We, as Christians, always need to be in spiritual training. We continually need to be using God's game plan (His word) to encourage and lead our friends down the narrow path of a championship life walking close to the Savior. If you think that a good cross-town rivalry game is exciting, try God's game...it's the best game goin.'

GROW! What ways can you train today for God's game in the upcoming season?

READY, *"We are fools for Christ's sake, but you are prudent in Christ;*
we are weak, but you are strong; you are distinguished, but we are
without honor." 1 Corinthians 4:10

SET, I know you've been on one end or the other of this beast
before. What might we be talking about here? Look what day it is.
Either you are planning or permitting (probably not by choice) a
joke for today, and you may not even know you are the victim. If
you are the culprit, be nice and do not embarrass the receiver. If
you *are* the receiver...take cover. Far too many times it seems that
the good guys always lose in this scene, and the bad guys (not really
bad) are the ones riding off into the sunset grinning on their trusty
horse.

All too often, we, as Christians, appear, from our perspective,
as the ones who look the fool in so many cases. Not cheating on a
test when everyone else is, not chiming in on a gossip session, not
going places we know will get us in trouble, not taking what is
being stolen, not acting on a date like what seems to be the norm,
and obeying your parents on curfew times, all can get us ridiculed.
I'm sure nine out of ten times the secular world looks at all this
Christian commitment and just snickers like the road-runner after
a Wylie Coyote flub. We may look like fools today, friend, but
we're not living for the moment, we're living for the kingdom to
come. Take notice, and notes (if you must), and realize that your
Savior Jesus looked like a fool too. He came into the world in a
barn and went out on a mountain of trash called Calvary while
hanging on a cross. Guess what? He also ascended into heaven to
prepare our beds in his house for our coming...now, that's what I
call a happy ending.

GROW! When did the world last view you as a fool for Christ?
How are you gonna' be seen today?

BATH TIME

READY, *"If we confess our sins, He is faithful and just to forgive us our sin and cleanse us from all unrighteousness." 1 John 1:9*

SET, There is no time more fun at my household than a home cooked supper, followed up with the priceless dessert of 'bath time.' The kids can hardly finish their last bite before they are dashing off up the stairs, leaving a trail of clothes, headed for that big warm bath filled with Mr. Bubble. I always thought (that is, until I had kids) that the sole goal for a bath was to get clean. The purpose, to my surprise, of baths is to experiment toys to see which float and which don't, how long it takes little brother to start kicking after holding him under for a new record, or what amount of water can be deposited in the floor before Dad gets mad. No matter how you've grown up, you'll probably always remember those tub-times, and if not, you will when the kiddos come.

So often in scripture you'll find a passage, word, or verse that you have heard so much that you become numb to it. This passage is one of those that you just glide right past as you fly through your quiet time. Do you see two mighty characteristics of God...faithful and just? Did you miss the part about what you have to do in order for Him to respond? How about... you confess your mistakes; He cleanses you. In John 13:10 Jesus explains to Peter, prior to the last supper and after He had washed Peter's feet, that there was not a need to take another bath (accept Christ as your Savior again). Just repent daily (wash your feet) to be cleansed and make things right with God. Wow, what a deal! How easy it is if we just stay soft at heart, He gives us our own 'bath time' of cleansing.

GROW! How often do you have a 'bath time' with God? Do you need a bath today?

SPUR 'EM ON

READY, *"And let us consider how to spur one another on to love and good deeds." Hebrews 10:24*

SET, Hey buckaroo, when was the last time you went to, or saw on the tube, a real live rootin'-tootin' western rodeo? (Well, that's too long.) A friend of mine is a real life rodeo cowboy who lives on a ranch, in a *Little House on the Prairie* look-a-like log cabin, with walls lined in trophy saddles and bookshelves displaying gold buckles of past arena victories. It is amazing that some folks view mounting up on a twelve hundred pound bull with sharp horns, or a crazy bucking horse, as a sport, but hey...some folks' pain tolerance is higher than other's, right? One time I asked him why, when riding a bucking bronc, he continued to run his spurs in the neck of this beast that was already mad enough to send a cowboy ballistic. He tilted his hat back, leaned against the bucking shoot, and proceeded to explain that one can make a pretty mellow horse into a champion bucker by spurring him on to a peak performance.

We live in a world which seems to always view things negatively. The art of stimulating or spurring on folks around us with a smile, brief note, or a soft, sincere word of encouragement seems to be classified as an 'endangered species.' As a disciple and ambassador (representative) of Jesus, you and I are to live a life different than that of the world. We (as a minority) are called to love our enemies and encourage others in a time when the majority says discourage and hate. What a different view would be seen of Christians if their army was one that didn't shoot the wounded, but helped them.

Today, you can either view a half cup of water as half full, or half empty. You see, it's all in the eyes of the viewer, not in the circumstance. Be a person who sees the good in others, and make it your goal to bring out the best in them. Go get 'em cowboy (or cowgirl) and let's make it a ride!

GROW! How can I spur someone on today? What specific ways can I do this?

READY, "For I know the plans I have for you, declares the Lord. Plans for welfare and not for calamity, to give you a future and a hope." Jeremiah 29:11

SET, One of the craziest things a person can be involved in is the designing and building of his dream home. It doesn't matter how big it is or how many bedrooms and baths it has; what matters is that it's your nest to which you fly home. I've built two homes in my life, been a part of designing a custom (never built before) home, and have actually chosen a contractor to carry out the plans put to a drafting table to produce a set of blueprints. I have helped from the beginning of the bulldozer knocking down trees, to the foundation of concrete load, to the framing, electrical, plumbing, drywall, roofing, all the way to the carpet laying. The number of details and hours of labor are incredible. Looking back when vision is twenty-twenty, I realize that the contractor plays a pivotal role in the final product...a house. It is so key that the builder knows how to read the plans and follows them to the detail of details.

Plans are funny things we attempt to live by daily. We make lots of them but seldom follow through with them. We schedule ourselves to death but rarely get the chance to fulfill our plans because of variables. It's nice to know that God, our Contractor, follows through with the plans He laid out on His drafting table at the beginning of time. What would it be like to have a God who _____ blueprints along the way with no grasp of the _____ on paper are to give vision for the future _____ a God who let menial things and variables _____ our lives? Our ways of building aren't nec-_____ our plans, His plans.

_____ence, when the final feature is presented it's _____ wait. Give God your plans (your heart and _____ back and watch the Creator build you into _____ designed you to be. One last thing, you _____ knows what He's doing. Remember, He's an expert in _____

GROW! In what ways do you feel nervous about your future? How strong is your faith in your Builder?

PLEASE

READY, "And without faith it is impossible to please Him, for he who comes to God must believe that He is, and that He is a rewarder of those who seek Him." Hebrews. 11:6

SET, I believe that teaching kiddos to say the word 'please' is as difficult as teaching them to sing *Jesus Loves Me* in Hebrew. No matter how young the teaching starts, it always seems like there is an echo in the house trying to train a five year old to say 'please' when he demands something. I do believe that sixty-five percent of my conversations with my kids (you'll see someday) somehow incorporate the word please.

Faith is such a tough concept to understand, especially when we live in such an intellectual world of 'for sures.' People for generations have tried to figure out what it means to have faith in something. It seems easier to have faith in a bungee cord, friends, car tires driving sixty-five miles an hour, bridges, airplanes, and skyscrapers than it does to have faith in God. Little do we realize that our foundation for future, our anchor of acceptance, our rock of righteousness all settle on faith...faith that Jesus is alive, He did die for my sins, He does love me unconditionally, He is returning, there is a life here after, the earth was created by Him, and so on.

We need to realize we cannot please Him without faith and we need it to live. There are many examples throughout the Bible which model for us how this is done, and what it takes to do it. Don't go to sleep tonight without hitting your knees and pleading with God to deepen and strengthen your faith in Him.

GROW! How deep is your faith today? What pleases God more, your works or faith in Him?

THE HEAT IS ON

READY, *"And don't be conformed to this world, but be transformed by the renewing of your mind, that you may prove what the will of God is, that which is good and acceptable and perfect."* Romans 12:2

SET, Can you feel it? It starts with a few butterflies, graduates to sweat, then comes the form of a knot deep in the pit of your stomach, and it climaxes with short breaths and tight muscles. What is this disease we are talking about? Pressure. It comes in all shapes and sizes and doesn't choose favorites for its victims. We find it around every corner of our lives. Through sports, education, business, medical fields, families and friends we feel it. One way or another, some time in your life, you *will* meet this beast, and you'll either defeat the foe or become clutched in its painful jaws. Pressure is something we all wish we could avoid, but when encountered and victoriously conquered, we realize the process feels better than winning any championship or earning any 'A.' Realizing that pressure can be a verb, not just a noun, and is a state mind, is winning half the battle.

When God created the heavens and the earth there probably weren't too many pressures that existed other than volcanic. That is until people were painted into the picture. He knew that people would pressure others into situations they wished had never existed. We call it 'peer' pressure, but I call it 'conforming' pressure. Nobody turns the heat up in our lives to conform to another image worse than friends. True friendship is a sacrificial love, not a conditional one. You were created in God's image, not the world's, and you do live in the world, but you're not of the world cuz' you're a new creature, remember? The best and only way to defeat the pest of pressure is to exterminate with God's purifying word daily.

Not too long ago Michael Jordan did a commercial that was really fun for Gatorade (which I love to drink), and the slogan was 'Be like Mike!' With no disrespect to Michael, I personally think I'll keep trying to be like Christ. It may not allow you to dunk, but it will win you victory in life.

GROW! What pressure do you face today? How are you going to defeat it?

A Taste Test

READY, *"Taste and see that the Lord is good." Psalm 34:8*

SET, One of the fondest memories I have from my childhood is Thanksgiving at my grandparents' house in Norman, Oklahoma. We would load up the old station wagon with my sisters' and my bikes on the roof and head across the Red River into Sooner country. Riding on the tractor with Grandpa, feeding the cows, and eating tender smoked turkey are vivid memories, but not so much as Grandma's homemade peach pies. I recall her spending hours working the crust, skinning the peaches and churning the ice cream. The phase I drooled over the most was after the pies were cooked, when she set them in the window sill to cool. Now to give you an idea of my situation, I was always about a smell away from those pies, but they were too high up in the window to reach. I remember getting a good swat (spanking) for stacking two barrels on top of each other and taking a pie (before dinner) and eating it all by myself. I might have been little, but I could eat. You better believe I knew how good they were, but my tastebuds had to taste and see for themselves to make sure.

You see, we all know that God is loving, powerful, merciful, gracious, protecting, tender, accepting, sacrificial, and almighty, *but* do we *really* know? The only way to know if He really is all He says He is, is to taste of Him and experience the satisfaction. Just as I knew Grandma's pies were good, I had to make the extra effort to go to them and try 'em out. The same is true with our God. You must taste and see of God's love, mercy, faithfulness, compassion, grace, and power. Take it from an expert in eating, taste and fulfillment definitely hold up to their billing.

GROW! When did you last taste of God? How do you really *taste* of Him? What desires will be satisfied when you do? Taste and see for yourself today.

40

READY, *"Wisdom comes from the abundance of wise (Godly) counsel." Proverbs 12:15*

SET, Nothing in our social system is given out as freely as advice. People will give it out for marriage, business deals, daily living, purchases, and tastes, without even the slightest attempt at thinking ahead of their words. You will find out for the rest of your life, we live among a people who rarely seek the right kind of biblically based counsel. There is a *huge* difference in advice and counsel. I'll make a gentleman's wager that at least two-thirds of the advice you receive today, and in the days to come, will have little regard for your best interest. If we made it a rule that everyone who gave advice must first give you a dollar (hit 'em where it hurts...in the pocketbook) every time they gave their airborne advice, things would be said less swiftly. Scripture tells us to be "slow to speak and quick to listen" for a definite reason.

Look again at this nugget of scripture found in the book of Proverbs. Do you see that there are several words which are key in the context? First of all, make sure your counsel comes from more than one person, in fact several persons. Second, make sure it's wise (Godly) counsel from sources who are walking with God on a daily basis. And lastly, make sure that it is not advice, but well thought out, pondered counsel which seeks to point you closer to your Savior. There are far too many of us who can find holes in the system and will seek counsel from the 'rubber stamp' people. In other words, these fellows are the ones who give us the answer we *want* but not necessarily what is right or what we *need.*

Get yourself your own personal 'board' of older individuals who think not as you do but are different, yet all follow the Savior sincerely. Use this group of folks to bounce off ideas, whims, thoughts or career moves. If a decision you're making affects your future, or others close to you, then give your board a call and ask them to think and pray about what the right answer is. Don't ask for a decision right then. This will take some preplanning, but give them time to seek God's counsel first and then get back to you. Remember, advice is *not* what you're after. God seeking counsel is.

GROW! When was the last time you let someone else in on your decision making? What type counsel do you give?

Gift Giving

READY, *"When He (Jesus) ascended into heaven, He led captive a host of captives and He gave gifts to men (women)." Ephesians 4:8*

SET, You're gonna' love this devo if you're one of those who wakes up early and runs with happy feet downstairs, before dawn, to open up presents on Christmas and to see if Santa stuffed your stocking. One of the greatest seasons we have on this planet is the celebration season of Jesus' birth when we get presents too. When was the last time you went to someone's birthday party and received more goodies than the birthday boy or girl? (Party favors don't count.) If and when you have children you will know what I'm talking about when I say the kiddos get 'excited'! If you're not planning to get married, you can relate because you were a child once. Christmas and all the festive frenzies that go along with this spirit are too few and far between. Wouldn't it be great to have this celebration of joy, when everyone's happy, caring, and full of turkey, each month? I'll take that idea back, because I'd be broke and weigh two tons if we did. So record over that message, will ya'? Jesus really is the reason for this spectacular season, and isn't it fun to be invited each year? There's nothing quite like giving and receiving fun things.

Jesus really does, through His Spirit, allow us to open gifts. His gifts. He has graciously given some to you (with no take-backs) to enjoy daily. What gifts am I speaking of? Spiritual gifts. In His family room He leaves, nicely wrapped for you to open and use daily, divine gifts for His glory. Your present may be the gift of giving, so give. The gift of mercy, so care. The gift of teaching, so train. The gift of exhortation, so encourage, or the gift of discernment, so choose. Whatever you find under God's giving tree, open it, use it, and be thankful. These gifts are like the EverReady Bunny...they keep going and going and going.

GROW! Do you open up your divine spiritual gift daily? Why or why not? How can you use it today?

THE VACCINE

READY, *"For all have sinned and fallen short of the glory of God being justified as a gift by His Grace through the redemption which is in Christ Jesus." Romans 3:23-24*

SET, Dr. Jonas Salk developed years ago a medical breakthrough when he finalized the phases of the polio vaccine. It might not mean too much to you now, but it did for thousands of people who were inflicted with this devastating disease. Today our country fears AIDS, cancer, Alzheimer's, heart conditions, and Multiple Sclerosis more than ever. The medical practice can't seem to find the cures. These ailments, like sin, break down our immune systems, and open us up to other viruses. The death of body and soul is wiping out our race right in front of our eyes.

The sickness we should fear the most in our nation is sin. Self remedies and vaccines are useless. Doctors can pass out prescriptions, but they are only dealing with the symptoms not the cause. When Jesus died and rose again, He alone showed the world this ancient plague passed down from Adam and Eve could only be beaten on His terms. He alone is the great physician and came up with the cure which was done at tremendous expense...His life.

The cross cured guilt, worry, lack of healthy self-image and eternal death for you and me, and showed a love like no other. The problem is that daily we pass by pedestrians who don't know there is a cure for eternal death. A vaccine is useless if people don't know it even exists. We can't continue to keep the cure in our pockets (hearts) and share it with no one because of a fear of rejection or an image problem. We are commanded to tell others of this Miracle Maker each and every day. Our world can't afford not to know any more.

GROW! When was the last time you told a non-Christian about Jesus? Why not tell someone today? What fears do you have?

How'd You Do Dat?

READY, "I am well content in my weaknesses with insult, with distress, with persecutions, with difficulties for Christ sake, for when I am weak then I am strong." 2 Corinthians 12:10

SET, Talented people in this county are as numerous as ticks on a coon dog. We are saturated with folks who are heads above any other western civilization. Athletically, technologically, educationally, militarily, socially, and politically, we are heads above anyone in our class. With talent running as thick as motor oil, our awareness of God's ultimate control over situations has diminished. Believe it or not, God *is* all knowing and *is* the ultimate producer of everything that occurs every second of our days. You are probably blessed with talents such as athletic ability, intellect, appearance (looks), and don't know where they may take you. Let me ask you a question...has anyone ever said, "How'd you do that?" after an accomplishment? In reality what they were saying was that they knew the limits of your abilities and talents and could see that you didn't have the tools to pull it off. Catch my drift?

What a spiritual victory it is when you bring an upset victory to the front page of your life's daily news. Those are the times you allow God to override your inadequacies to produce a standing ovation performance. Those are the times when your world has fallen apart and the pieces are lost, yet you allow Him to pull it all together to finish the puzzle in style. In the midst of turbulence, turmoil, and trials, you draw on God to help you survive the crash and land your life safely. There will be peer persecution, verbal tongue lashings, and harassment of humans, but to come through the manure piles of mankind smelling like a rose is a credit to God's loving kindness. It will be those weak times of your life that God can make you as strong as a steel beam. So next time someone says, "How'd you do that?", simply smile and say, "I had a good coach."

GROW! When was the last time you were weak? How did you react? Did or didn't you use God? What will you do next time?

RESPECTED REPUTATION

READY, "*You shall follow the Lord your God and fear Him, and you shall keep His commandments, listen to His voice, serve Him, and cling to Him.*" *Deuteronomy 13:4*

SET, Fear is an obsolete word when you park it and think it over. Webster's Dictionary sums it up best..."an uneasy feeling that something may happen contrary to one's desires." These words became reality not long ago when a group of folks loaded up the van and drove to the Nantahala River, which means 'land of the noonday sun' in the language of the Cherokee. This roaring river of rapids lies close to the small town of Bryson City, North Carolina and is outlined by the Smokey Mountains. It was there we tried our hand (or paddles) at kayaking a real live river. The river was a brisk fifty degrees (no Bahama water, that's for sure) and is dam released, which means it's dry at nights. The riverbed gradient averages thirty-eight feet per mile in the seven and three quarter mile long stretch to Wesser (a town). The Class Twelve white water is virtually non-stop, easing up a little before the true test...Nantahala Falls. You pass boulders, downed trees and dive through named rapids of churning water called 'Four Eddy Rapid,' 'Whirlpool,' 'Devil's Kitchen,' 'The Quarry,' etc. 'til you reach the outdoor center after surviving the falls. It was here I learned what 'fear for your life' really meant in English. I'll tell you this much, I floated upside down over many rocks and saw much marine life on this expedition. What exactly were my fears? Well, drowning comes to mind, or maybe being swallowed by a whirlpool. No matter what you call the emotion, I called it scared stiff.

When we look at the comparative sizes of the Old and New Testament, we see the Old is two-thirds of the entire Bible. One key phrase, seen as often as pollution, is the phrase 'fear the Lord.' Does that mean be intimidated? Frightened? Horrified? Unloving? Or does it mean *respect* for our Creator? You see, I fear the river, but that doesn't stop me from going back and kayaking it again. Fear is a word we misinterpret. You are to come to your Father in heaven with respect and honor. Just as the river is mighty in power, so is God, but He gives you His love as the door to enter.

GROW! What do you fear most in life? Why? How do you view God today?

READY, Whoever drinks of the water that I shall give him shall never thirst; the water that I shall give him shall become in him a well of water springing up to eternal life." John 4:14

SET, You won't have to look too far, in fact about as far as it is to your local *Git 'n Go*, to find a rack of bottled water. I'm not sure if it was for health or status reason, but one thing is for sure, it's a hit. Bottled water is as common at games, social events, and wedding receptions as hot dogs are at baseball games. Some buy it by the convenient hand-held size, and others rent the dispenser and make it a permanent fixture in their homes. It's definitely here to stay and if you haven't gotten hooked yet, look out, because you soon will.

I'm sure that if Jesus was an entrepreneur, He would have bottled the water He is talking about in this verse, and would have made a few bucks double quick. In Christ's time, water was not only tough to find, but a valuable commodity for folks. The witness, John, narrates his version of the Samaritan women and Jesus' conversation at the well. Jesus takes a necessity of life, then and now, to illustrate a valuable lesson in life. He shows you that water, a huge percentage of our physical make-up is comparable to Himself. He states that if you drink of the substance of water, you will thirst again, but if you drink of Christ, the real thirst quencher (no, it wasn't *Gatorade*, either), that you will never thirst again. In fact, it will be a live well that arrives in heaven. Wow! What a deal, no more stops on the trail for a water break. Jesus purified, crystal clear liquid will be all you need to sustain life hereafter. Look out Evian, move over Ozarka, here comes Jehovah Water.

GROW! When was the last time you drank of Christ? How can He make you thirst no more? What sort of things do you thirst after?

Expressing Individuality

READY, *"I will give thanks to thee, for I am fearfully and wonderfully made; wonderful are thy works, and my soul knows it very well."* Psalms 139:14

SET, When in doubt, blame it on a low self-image, right? It seems like everybody who is anybody wants a scapegoat, so we have chosen the old self-worth. The problem with not only non-believers, but Christians too, is that we don't see like God sees. A friend of mine, a very talented Christian singer name Billy Sprague, sings a song with catchy lyrics that say "I am as I am if I am all I see, but if He is all I see then I see me as He" (confusing, isn't it?). Anyway...the gist of it simply states that when we put our focus on the Creator and not the creation (me), then the fog of worthlessness is lifted.

Get this...you need to be taking a victory lap not singin' the blues about you as a valuable vessel. You need to be spending less time trying to revamp the system and more time sharpening up what and who you are. Listen to me for one minute, and I promise you I won't stutter and make sure your ears don't flap, but you *are wonderfully made!!!* Okay, was that loud enough for ya'? Let me clue your brain in to this wave too...God *don't make junk!!!* Hear that too? We all, including myself, should jump out of bed like a missile off the launch pad, throw our hands up heavenward and say, "thanks a ton, God, for making me like me." What a new outlook on life, not having to be something your not. If you're created to be a duck then *don't* try to be like your neighboring squirrels (ducks look stupid climbing trees and squirrels look even dumber swimming). Before you go to bed tonight I want you to read this verse ten times and try to memorize it (oh no, homework, dude!), cuz' it's worth your time.

GROW! Do you know deep in your soul that you are a wonderful creation? Do you feel like a castle or a shack? According to this verse, what did God create? Do you believe it?

47

READY, *"He who pursues righteousness and loyalty finds life, righteousness and honor." Proverbs 21:21*

SET, It is seen on the Disney movies, noticed it at the city park on a summer day, and admired in the duck blind while hunting. See what? Notice what? Admire what? The loyalty of a dog. Isn't it strange that we need an animal with four paws to model for us this valuable trait? It's a list fart in society today. It's not found in many businesses, friendships, or nations. Where has it gone? Why has this great quality fallen extinct? It's the glue which holds together a company, it's the mortar that bonds a relationship in a marriage, and it's the adhesive that grips our relationship with our Savior.

If you study the life and qualities of Jesus, you'll see a golden thread which runs through almost every parable, miracle, and teaching...loyalty. How loyal to you was Jesus? Let's say to death! That's right, read the most widely memorized scripture in society today, John 3:16, and see if loyalty jumps out at you and grabs you by the throat. Jesus died first because of His loving loyalty to His Father in Heaven, then for you and me. Daily you have the opportunity to be or not to be (I'm not talking of a wedding vow) loyal to some person, place, or Savior (you thought I was gonna say thing). Begin today. It's never too late to start to draw upon the divine power of God Almighty to begin to instill in you the valuable quality of loyalty. You'll be amazed how far this ticket will take you on the journey of life. Let's come up with our own catchy marketing slogan...'*Christians, Laborers of Loyalty*' (look out Nike). Be as loyal to others as a dog is to its owner.

GROW! How loyal are you? What sort of things are you loyal to? How can you become more loyal today?

READY, *"But thanks be to God, who always leads us in His triumph in Christ, and manifests through us the sweet aroma of the knowledge of Him in every place." 2 Corinthians 2:14*

SET, Doctors tell us that our brains have the power to recall memories through our senses. In other words, you have the capability to remember from your past experiences certain events, places or persons by the sense of smell. There are certain fragrances that when caught by your nose, will send a message to your computer (brain) and bring back a specific memory where the same smell existed. When God created us, He didn't leave out one detail on His final product.

Did you realize that Jesus living your heart will produce an aroma communicating a knowledge of Him in *every* place? Don't walk past the triumph. God leads His family members, shepherding them like sheep, to a victory, not defeat. God also is the creative force behind this far reaching fragrance which He alone produces. We as Christians can be anywhere at any time and can send out a fragrance that beats the heck out of any popular perfumes the stores have to sell.

You have the privilege of setting off either an unpleasant odor of worldliness or a pleasant perfume of purity. What an awesome responsibility we are given to represent our Savior in a community of environmentally unsafe smog. So, go do your part, because this is one emission that won't damage the ozone.

GROW! If your friends were to compare you to a fragrance, which one would it be?

ALL STRESSED UP

READY, *"And which of you by being anxious can add a single cubit to your life's length?" Luke 12:25*

SET, Have you ever been 'all dressed up' and had nowhere to go? What an awful feeling it is to be doing something with no final act to look forward to. Recently my wife was driving and saw an ad on a Houston, Texas billboard for a counseling center which read, "All *stressed* up and no place to go." What a terrible predicament to be in with so little hope. The problems you face today are going to multiply like rabbits in ten years. The older you get, the more you'll clue in that life gets harder, not easier with age. Relationships, grades, eager moments, career decisions, etc. are going to become more complicated with marriage, job pressures, children, financial obligations, and more. Stress will be with you as long as a loyal dog. You can run but you can't hide from its teeth of tension, paws of pressure, and bite of the beast. So, what do I do to conquer this beast?

First of all, you don't go down to the local bookstore for a formula of self-help. If you could help yourself, you wouldn't be dealing with this problem in the first place. You take it on home to God. That's right, the stress snubber-outer is what I call Him. He takes your problems off your hands and bears the load like a heavy suitcase in a long airport terminal. Now you might be saying I'm crazy and that I'm one sandwich short of a picnic, but I've seen results in this plan. You can, too. Talk to God like you would your best friend and take it (your problem) to the foot of the cross, drop it, and leave it. God is in the business of problem solving, and it will free you up to be '*not* all stressed up and *someplace* to go.'

GROW! How do you handle stress? What stresses you out the most? What sort of problems do you feel God really can't handle?

BEING LOST

READY, *"For the Son of Man (Jesus) has come to seek and save that which is lost." Luke 19:10*

SET, Have you ever been lost as a little kid in a mall, grocery store, or stadium, isolated from friends or family? What a terrible, traumatic experience this can be at a young age. I personally thought after the age of sixteen (the age of freedom to drive), that this fear would be forgotten...until Idaho.

At the age of thirty-five I was invited by a close friend to go on a hunting trip in Idaho, on the middle fork of the Salmon River, in a five million acre wilderness. The only way in and out was by horseback, and we were forever away from the nearest paved road or town with any sort of population. Animals of all shapes and sizes, some had never seen a human, existed in large numbers. There in the mountains, I somehow lost my bearings and got separated from my party with no food, water, or matches to survive. I can't explain adequately with words the fear that overtook me, as I searched frantically for anyone who walked on two feet. My emotions could have been measured like the magnitude of a California earthquake. After about two hours of walking up, down and all around, I sat down and began to make some deals with God. I have never, to this day, experienced anything quite like the fear as a grown man lost, and never choose to experience it again.

Do you realize how many people you pass every minute of your life who are lost in the wilderness of eternity? How hopeless one begins to feel while contemplating never being found and dying just a memory. We have been, one might say, chosen by God to be His Rescue Team for the lost souls of this world. Finding a lost, unsaved being and leading him home (salvation) is one of the most precious experiences you will ever know. Sharing the Savior of your soul to a wanderer in the wilderness is better than any rush this world could ever deliver. Do your part and find someone. Take it from me, it's great to be found.

GROW! When was the last time you shared Jesus with someone lost? Why not today?

REAL MEN

READY, *"Our attitude among you was one of tenderness."*
1 Thessalonians 2:7

SET, Okay, I need to ask, if you are of the female species, to pass right on by this devo, unless you'd like a peep into understanding the male gender. This devo is targeted at the 'real men' which wander around in this world.

Ask yourself this...what is a 'real man' today? Who fits the mold of a hero to you? As I ask my own self these questions, I realize how much my answers have evolved through the years over this rocky road. When you think of the subject of manhood you might bring to mind John Wayne, Rambo, Steven Segal, a Busch Beer mountain man, Michael Jordan, General 'Stormin' Norman' Schwarzkopf, Elvis, and the list could go on forever. Why is it that society instead of scripture has shaped our thinking on this subject? There is a real problem when we define 'manhood' by the opinions of contemporary 'experts.' Manliness is not a cosmetic costume but an inward characteristic. Manhood started in the Garden of Eden and has rapidly deteriorated since the fall. Gary Smalley, the king of visual word pictures, would be proud of this one to explain what men look like... "A steel rod wrapped in velvet.' That's right, read it again (it's worth a double take). Imagine a rough, tough, rigid metal piece of scrappy iron neatly covered in soft, sensitive, caring velvet.

Jesus, once again, is the ultimate example of a conquering king, unwavering warrior, human hero, and faithful friend. He continually focused in on a purpose and goal (men are natural conquerors) yet attacked them with care and kindness. Manliness is nothing but a son of God (you) determined to give his all with no compromise of integrity. Don't feel defeated at the realization that you might not be matching up (don't feel alone, we're all there). Like they say, the best time to start on something is now, so lets get started. Let's show this topsy-turvy backwards world that are still some *real men* on this planet; men with a heart for God and His ways.

GROW! Who is your hero? Why? What can you do today that will allow you to be a 'Man of God'?

IRON ON IRON

READY, "*Iron sharpens iron, so one man sharpens another.*" *Proverbs 27:17*

SET, Have you ever wondered why God didn't put each one of us on a planet of our own? I mean, hey, it's not like the universe in which we live doesn't have enough outer space places for us to live. Wouldn't it be cool to phone up a friend and tell him that your new address is 1124 East Venus, or Apartment 4 Jupiter Drive? Why ask why? (Don't tell what pagan commercial I stated that from.)

If you've never been to a blacksmith's metal working shop, you've missed out. The shop is full of scrap-iron piles, seventy five pound anvils, coal burning furnace, and lots of metal mallets. It's amazing to watch a true blacksmith mastering an old piece of black metal into a piece of art. When heated, the smith can force, bend, pound, torque and flatten any piece of iron into a useful tool. It's awesome to see that an iron hammer can contour an iron rod into a knife, a fireplace set, or dinner bell. Two of the same materials can function for the same goal in the end.

No matter what you do or make your career, you will deal with people (iron). This world goes round because of common folks just like you and me. God placed us in the mortal madness for a distinct purpose and that is to be sharpened and shaped into a better person. Iron *does* sharpen iron. We, at times, would like to 'beam me up, Scotty' and get the fat out of Dodge to escape this process, but we can't. You won't always see things the same way, have the same opinion, agree with a plan, like the same movies, date or marry the same type person, enjoy the same sports, read the same books, like the same foods, listen to the same music as others you come in contact with. God made each of us different and unique for a reason (praise God), and we should learn to appreciate and admonish our differences, *not* condemn them. So the next time you're about to blow a lid because someone doesn't see as you see, remember this, they are 'no better, no worse, just different' (NBN-WJD).

GROW! What type people rub you the wrong way? Why? How can you learn to appreciate them?

PRAYER PROPOSAL

READY, *"For those things which you pray and as believe that you have received them and they shall be given to you." Mark 11:24*

SET, Now this is *not* gonna' be one of those devos on 'name it, claim it.' This devo is on a kind of prayer warrior who has the right perspective and procedure. I'll begin with a true story I heard in a small farming community in western Iowa. As usual, the good ol' American farmer was being dealt another bad hand in the weather department. There had been a total of thirty-one days without a drop of rain, so a town meeting was called. The location was the local church with the preacher presiding. The gathering was basically a prayer meeting to ask God to show favor on their dry, scorched farm land and crops so they could have a good harvest to pay some bills. The reason this meeting and story are so interesting is that *all* the locals who attended the meeting came umbrellas. Now that's what I call an expectant prayer meeting.

We, as Christians, only have one road to travel to see the Savior, and that's on 'Highway Prayer.' The only communication we have with the Creator is through the two-way radio we call prayer. With all that in mind, isn't it important that we know *how* to pray? God will always answer your requests with either yes, no, or wait. What we need to do more of is to get our tuner tuned to God so finely that our prayers match His way of thinking. This way, when we pray, we are so deeply into God's will and looking out for His best interest, all our requests and petitions are right on. Now what this does is give us the liberty to pray boldly through faith that we will receive His will for the particular situation we're praying for. Whether it's healing someone sick, a material matter, guidance on a decision, or wisdom in our thinking, He will come through....bank on it.

So, be like that group of believers in Iowa and pray to God with results in mind...cuz' when it rains, it pours!

GROW! Who or what can you pray for today? When you pray, do you pray believing God is listening? Do you pray consistently? Do you doubt you're righteous enough for God to listen?

CARRY-ON LUGGAGE

READY, *"Jesus said 'Anyone who does not carry his own cross and follow me cannot be my disciple.'" Luke 14:27*

SET, The young man was frankly at the end of his rope. Seeing no way out, he dropped to his knees in prayer saying, "Lord, I just can't go on." He continued, saying, "I have too heavy a cross to bear." The Lord replied, "My son, if you cannot bear its weight, just place your cross inside this room, then open that other door and pick out any cross you wish." The young man, filled with relief said, "Thank you a ton, God," then sighed and did as he was told. Upon entering the other door he saw many crosses, some so big that the tops weren't visible. All of a sudden he spotted a small cross leaning against the far wall. "I'd like that small one, Lord." The Lord replied, "My son, that's the cross you just brought in."

Trials are kinda' like a giant fourteen thousand foot mountain that looks small from an airplane...until you land and try to hike up that puppy. The cross that God our Father has asked us to carry is gonna' feel heavy and burdensome at times. The stress of carrying it will sometimes drop you to your knees (it did Jesus too). Take courage and tap into God's power and might to continue on. If you want to be a true modern day disciple of Christ, you're gonna' get sore muscles, weak knees, and be humbled daily. That's okay though, because your labor is not in vain, nor is your pain. A quick thought about this cross carrying stuff...where are you carrying it to? The answer is, the same place Jesus did...to your death; and realize it's a one way trip to Calvary. The next time you feel too faint to go on, look around you and see other's struggling with their own crosses, bigger and smaller. Jesus just tells us to press on!

GROW! When was it toughest for you to carry your cross? Have you ever wished you could chunk your cross? What stopped you? How can we learn that we all have a cross to bear and none is easy or light?

READY, *"Enlarge the place of your tent, stretch out the curtains of your dwellings, spare not, lengthen your cords and strengthen your pegs." Isaiah 54:2*

SET, My philosophy on life is this: There dwells among us two types of folks, those who read stories and those who make stories. I love those people who are spunky and spontaneous enough to step out and do something totally opposite to their personalities. For those who like living life by a thread and on the edge, that steppin' out may mean sitting down to read and pray for a whole afternoon in the country. For those more conservative, it may mean getting out, letting their hair down, and going hiking, bungee jumping (not!), or whatever. What I'm trying to say is the same thing that the prophet Isaiah is saying... *branch out!* The life we live in this earth suit is too short to not step out of our comfort zones and try something a little different. Obviously, this wild hair needs to be done in the framework of God's word, but once you've been okayed for take-off, then fire up those after-burners and take air.

You will notice that branching out will cause a spiritual turn of your faith. When we step out, we are going beyond our limits, out-punting our coverage, or competing out of our league. God loves those times when we come to the end of self and to the beginning of Savior. Go ahead with it then, broaden the borders of your tent (life) and experience those uncharted regions. Make a story today for God and this world to read from you life...it will be on the best seller list, I bet.

GROW! What legal thing have you always wanted to do but never did? What are those regions of life which make you feel uncomfortable? How deep is your faith? Can it be deeper? What can you do different this week to deepen your faith?

READY, *"Thy word is a lamp unto my feet and a light unto my path." Psalm 119:105*

SET, When most of us hear this verse we immediately recall Amy Grant singing the song. You've heard if for years in church, youth groups and on the radio but have you ever stopped and looked at it? It comes off as a pretty simple set of divine words which have a nice ring to them and they fit well with musical notes. Read it one time through, and your report would be that the Bible is like a light to my steps along this Christian journey, right? Well, pretty close, but look again...notice a key word in this verse? No, it's not lamp or light, but 'feet.' Check this bad boy thought out for a minute. God's word is a light, but its halo only surrounds your steps. Get it? Okay, I'll explain further...when you are walking down a narrow path at night with a flashlight pointed downward, you can only see a few feet (no pun intended) ahead of you at a time. In other words, you still need to walk with care (slowly, one step at a time) or you'll run into a tree, or stumble on an unnoticed boulder. I mean, if God wanted to, He could light up the country side with His word so you wouldn't even need a lamp. Come on now, this is God who can do it all, right?

The Bible is the flame in the lamp that gives light to every step our feet walk on this thin, windy pathway we call Christianity. I believe God is telling us that hey, the Bible is great, but it's not enough to make this journey...we still need His Spirit to guide us, too. He's telling us we must still carry faith in the Father accompanied by a lamp (not a spotlight) to find our way through life's dark, messed-up world in which we all travel. Study the word of God daily to keep that flame from going out, and also keep the faith which compliments His word. Don't be afraid of the danger which *will* lie ahead...you forget, Jesus made the path and has been on it several times before you.

GROW! How often do you read the Bible? Why don't you read it daily? Do you believe it is a lamp to your feet? How can you get excited about God's word? How can you make Bible study a habit?

You're Acting Childish

READY, *"When I was a child, I used to speak as a child, think as a child, reason as a child; but when I became a man (mature), I did away with childish things." 1 Corinthians 13:11*

SET, Have you ever sat back and taken a gander (look) at how our society is set up? Kids are doing those kid things, adolescents are doing the teenage things, and adults are doing those adult things. Kids are walking in diapers, riding bikes, building forts, playing with dolls, jumping rope, and picking their noses. Teenagers are checking out the opposite sex, hot-rodding the cars, manicuring the nails, deciding on colleges, cramming for tests, playing the sports, and still (more discretely) picking their noses. Lastly the adults are going to work, raising the kids, meeting deadlines, taking vacations, playing more gold, setting up wills, managing the assets, caravaning to the games, cleaning the house, mowing the lawn, and getting more gray hair. This civilization, whether you realize it or not, grows you up naturally. We all graduate from diapers to dialect, project to progress, hand-me-downs to honeymoons without ever giving it a second glance.

The natural system grows people up, but the spiritual curriculum takes studying and effort on our own part. We have in our Christian circles today adult babies. Now I don't mean that in a demeaning way, just factual. We grow up in every way but in our faith. What would it look like if a forty year old person went back to a third grade classroom to learn to read and write...silly. You will look pretty silly, too, if you have been a 'true Christian' for twenty years but still walk and talk like you're a babe. Maturing and growing up in our faith means doing things as Christ would, not as our old nature does. It means taking on the divinely injected characteristics of our Creator which makes us salt and light. It means seeing situations, circling circumstances, living the unlovable, taming the tongue, terminating the thoughts, and walking the way we should. We need to grow up in Christ just like we grow up in life. We need to mature in wisdom like we mature in years. Come on, grow away those childish conducts and ripen in righteousness.

GROW! Have you done away with childish ways? Why or why not? How can you practically do this?

58

READY, "I have fought the good fight, I have finished the course, I have kept the faith." 2 Timothy 4:7

SET, During the summer Olympics, watching Ben Johnson and Carl Lewis, two world class sprinters going head to head in the 100 meter sprint, I remember the TV commentator just ranting and raving about the start of this run and its importance. Johnson was known for his explosive start to the point that both feet were literally off the ground at once when he blasted off the blocks toward the finish line. Lewis, on the other hand, was a slow starter (almost last out), yet his strength of speed was in the last 30 meters of the race. What a run of two fleet of feet it was!

In life, so many people make such a big deal about the beginning and not the ending. Focus seems to have finished on the start and not the tape at the end of the race. Isn't it ironic that the winner is not determined by the first out of the starting blocks but down the track at the timer table? Consistency and perseverance seem to have lost their way in our list of needed character qualities in today's trends. Isn't it more important to celebrate a fifty year wedding anniversary, or twenty years on a job, or receiving a diploma? Yes, the starting blocks and the beginning are important, *but* not as important as the finishing. God calls us to a trip that is going to take time and endurance to complete. This scripture stresses the importance of fighting the fight, finishing the race, and keeping the faith throughout. You *are* a runner; you *are* a participant; you *are* a starter, and you are *able* to finish with Christ as your strength (in your heart and legs). Go ahead, take off the warm-up, stretch out, crawl into the blocks, and focus on the finish.

GROW! What enables us to finish the race strong? How can you train to endure?

GUARANTEES

READY, "So much the more also Jesus has become the guarantee of a better covenant." Hebrews 7:22

SET, There is not too much you can buy these days that doesn't come with some sort of guarantee. Living in a free enterprise system, as you might imagine, there is a varied length on all guarantees, but for the most part they're pretty reasonable. At times, we might choose one product over another, both the same price, because of a better guarantee. Whether you're buying a watch, telephone, bike, microwave, car, video game, or new set of snow tires (inside humor), you'll be looking for a good guarantee on the future performance of the product. A guarantee is nothing more than a pledge that something will meet stated specifications or that a specific act will be performed or your money back. The reason that we all like this little written code of warrant is because it gives us a sense of security.

In life we are all looking for that same set of standards on products to apply to our lives. We want the security that an insurance policy of life-time guarantees bring us, but the problem is that it's a false sense of security. I mean, come on, why don't airlines guarantee your safe arrival or your money back? Why don't coaches guarantee a championship, or pastors guarantee a fiftieth anniversary at the wedding? Because they cannot be absolutely sure that they can deliver the goods. In English...there are no, I repeat, (I didn't stutter with my pen), no guarantees in life that are a done deal except that Jesus is your ticket to eternity. Now, what part of the word ënoí don't you understand?

GROW! Why is security in life so important? What makes you feel secure? Is your security in places, persons, or things, or is it in Jesus? Can you think of one guarantee in life that is truly valid?

BEING CHILDISH

READY, *"Truly I say to you, unless you have child-like faith, it is impossible to inherit the kingdom of heaven." Matthew 18:3*

SET, Few times, to none, has a perfect stranger pranced up to me, whipped out a pencil and paper, and asked me for my autograph. Now, on the other hand, it's part of daily rituals for the likes of Michael Jordan, Jackie Joyner Kersey, Cindy Crawford, Emmitt Smith, Bonnie Blair, the President of the United States, Michael Jackson, and the list goes on. Let me tell you about my biggest fan of all time...my son. To him I am someone famous who can do no wrong. I don't break world records, model for *Vogue*, have my picture in *Sports Illustrated*, or run a nation. I do far more important stuff like fix training wheels, unscrew jars with crayons in them, catch crickets and snakes with my bare hands, mow the yard, and do cheerleading stunts with his mom in the living room. To my kids I can do it all. Little do they understand that most of what I do, anyone with two legs could do. They say, "Wow, Daddy you're so strong," when I'm not, or "My Dad is faster than a plane," when if I went any slower, I'd be in reverse. Are you catching my point here? My children think I'm 'great' because they depend on me for *all* the small things of a functioning little person's life. With dependence comes faith in what or who is being depended on.

How much do you depend on your Father (God) for the small things of life, daily? Gang, when you revert back to depending on God for your smallest needs (i.e. tests in class, friendships, dates) then you will see God as He desires to be seen. Watching the faith of children is an incredible sight to see. At the age of four, my son jumped off a roof top to me and would do the same again today. Why? Because I have never dropped him. So why shouldn't he trust me, he has no reason to believe otherwise? Your Father in heaven wants you to jump to Him, because He never has, and never will, drop you. Dependability is a dying quality in society today, and believe you me, it's great to depend on Someone who is bigger and stronger than we are, to seek refuge in His big open, loving, caring, tender arms daily...for the small things too. So come on, and be a kid again! Just see again how great your Savior really is.

GROW! How dependent are you on God? What today do you have going you could give to Him to handle?

61

Hero Shopping

READY, *"Everyone, after he has been fully trained, will be like his teacher." Luke 6:40*

SET, It doesn't take long in the riches of society to find poverty in this profession. The problem is that there are not many folks interviewing for this job because of the incredible amount of experience needed. First, one must be willing, a person of integrity, honesty, loyalty, unselfish, humble, dedicated, caring, self-disciplined, and intent on one purpose (I could go on). Wow! What a resume' would be needed in this job search. Isn't it funny that the profession we're talking about is the endangered species of real life, red, white and blue 'heroes'? Isn't it ironic (look closely) that the qualities mentioned don't deal with head knowledge but heart knowledge? Believe it or not (no, it's not Ripley's), very few heroes or mentors are around to be followed. In this profession, the title must be earned, it's not just freely given. Worthiness must be proven on the playing fields of family relationships, battle grounds of business, spectrum of sports, and the stadiums of society.

As you grow older, you will observe that trying to find this mentor is like trying to find a penny in the Grand Canyon. They come around about as often as a total eclipse of the sun, but guess what? They *are* out there in small numbers and not where you expect to see them. They carry no flash (they're humble), they wave not their own banner (unselfish), nor do they advertise their position (folks of integrity). The truth is, the position can only be held by a sincere follower of Jesus. Why? Without Him there is no divine strength to pull off walking upright day after day, year after year. If you want to find a hero, start first, not by looking for one, but by praying for one. God wants us all to have a mentor to teach us (like Paul did Timothy), and then wait on the Lord.

Let me offer a brief suggestion as you climb this mountain in search of a glimpse of this endangered species. See if they can say these simple, yet convicting words, "you can do as I do." But, first make sure they are an original and not a cheap replica of a real, live, modern day 'hero.'

GROW! Who is your hero today? Can you do as they do? Is what they do honoring to God?

READY, "*This world has blinded the minds of the unbelieving, that they might not see the light of the gospel of the glory of Christ, who is the image of God*" 2 Corinthians 4:4

SET, Nationwide, one of the biggest battles that goes on day after day, season after season, is over the thermostat. It seems to me, men are more thick skinned, and women more thin skinned. Therefore, they can't agree on a common temperature setting. I know that the gender issue is not true of everyone, because some folks are just hot natured and others cold natured, 'N.B.N.W.J.D.' (which means after interpretation 'no better, no worse, just different'). As a child my little sister, (who is now a genius), used to tell me "Stop changing the thermometer, the house is freezing." and I'd reply, "Hey goofy, it's a thermostat." You see, the difference is that one tells the temperature, yet the other dictates it. The common thread is that they both deal with temperature.

Here's a crazy analogy for ya.' Whether you're a follower of Christ or not, you were born into this world (this is the given, the temperature). Some people let the world dictate their thoughts, actions, decisions, and attitudes, and they are the thermometers. Now, on the other hand, there are those who dictate the temperature around them through setting the pace, by example, for the thoughts, actions, decisions and attitudes of folks they come in contact with (the thermostat). Here is an interesting thought to bubble your brain cells over. Just what can you control in your life? Answer...only yourself. Another bubbler—can you control others? Answer...no. Dictators have tried but wound up with revolutions on their hands.

It's a goofy illustration, I know, but I think the point is proven. Yes, you have the daily ability to not be influenced by this wicked world but help in the prevention of decay by simply deciding. You are what you are, because Jesus made you what you are...don't forget it!

GROW! What are you, a thermostat or thermometer? What do you want to be? How can you do that?

READY, *"I am confident of this very thing, that He who began a good work in you will perfect it until the day of Christ Jesus"* Philippians 1:6

SET, Talk about a buzz word for the '90's. You'll hear the word 'status quo' used more in describing a person, place or thing, and as often as you hear the words 'politically correct.' I'm about as bright as a two watt light bulb, so I had to look up what this 'hip' word meant. It means a condition or state in which a person or thing is or has been stuck in. A few years back we used an uncool word to describe a similar expression: stereotype. This good old country of ours seems to 'tag' people as a certain way or classify them in a category and it's heck to get out from under that label. If you personally haven't been labeled, I'm sure you have seen it performed. You know, someone is overweight, so they're a slob, skinny, so they're a wimp, big, then they're dumb as a rock, don't make A's, so they're retarded, don't drive a Lexus, so they're poor; have a nice house, then they're a rich snob, don't have a pretty face or perfect teeth, so they're ugly, and so on.

Why do we do this to others or allow it to be done to us? There is a huge, loving, caring God who desires to inject His working Spirit in us to help make us better and transform us to be more like His Son. People fear God because they are afraid of Him judging them harshly. The funny (really sad though) thing is that we judge ourselves and others more harshly than He does. We pass personal judgment then condemn to the seller of self-image. Status quo is a phase we pass through on life's journey, yet we don't have to reside in it. We don't need to park there, we can put our lives in drive with God at the wheel and watch Him pull off miracles in areas we fail in. A good friend on mine always says, "it is no secret what God can do, but it's sure fun to watch Him pull it off." Go ahead...punt the status quo and let God pull off some miracles in your life. Don't settle for second best.

GROW! In what areas of your life do you feel you're stuck in the status quo? What practical ways can you and God improve through them? What does stereotyping do to a person's self-image?

A PERSONAL PUMP

READY, "*I am the way, the truth, and the life. No one comes to the Father except through me." John 14:6*

SET, One of the many hobbies I enjoy, along with thousands of others, is biking. There are few better methods known to mankind for seeing the scenery and getting the old heart rate up than jumping on a bike and pounding the pedals. Not long ago I went on a Saturday afternoon ride of about twenty miles with some buddies of mine. I was well equipped with my 'skid lid' in place (my helmet) and a few tools accompanied by a spare tube. About ten miles down the road I noticed my ride getting tougher and a slight wobble in my rear (tire, that is). I glanced down to find I had a flat. I pulled off the road (that's best for your safety) before I became a road rash and began to fix my tire. I opened my tool pouch and went to work like a pit crew on an Indy car. After the tube was in place, I began to pump up the tire to get me back in working order. I pumped and pumped but with little success in filling the tire. Finally, I noticed that the tube valve had to be unscrewed before the air could flow into the tube. (Darn those fancy Italian tubes.)

How many popped pedestrians, who fail to open their heart valve to a good pumping up of the knowledge of Christ, do we see all around us? God could have designed us (remember, He's God) with no valve (our will) at all, but He didn't. He didn't make us robots but gave us the option of opening our lives to Him in response to his invitation. God doesn't force His ways or His lifestyle on us. He lets us find our own way (remember, He knocks at our door but doesn't kick it down). Open up your heart and mind to the truths of our Creator who cares if we ride again. Don't allow the debris of this world to let the air out of your life without having a spare ready to replace and fill with God's breath of life. Go ahead, ride on!

GROW! Why did God allow us to keep our 'wills?' How do you submit to God? Why is our God a jealous one? How can you pump someone up today? Will you?

READY, *"For kings and all who are in authority, in order that we may lead a quiet and tranquil life in all godliness and dignity."* 1 Timothy 2:2

SET, If you want to take a trip you could classify as educational, you might try 'The Big Apple.' You know, home of the Mets, Broadway shows, population seven million, Wall Street, subways, Statue of Liberty, thirty dollar taxi rides, Central Park, Madison Square Garden, Time Square, LaGuardia Airport, World Trade Center, Queens, Macy's, Trump Towers, Plaza Hotel (where *Home Alone* was filmed), and on and on. Never in my life have I been in a place where I felt like I had been 'beamed up' on the Starship Enterprise and relocated to another planet. It's a concrete jungle of huge skyscrapers and conversation is muffled by tourists and taxis. I learned more in my three day stay in New York City than I did in twenty-two years of school.

A stunning thought to realize is that even in Christ's day among the multitudes, Jesus saw the benefits of mellow times in the mountains. The forethought and wisdom that flows from scripture is refreshing to apply in our modern daily lives. How important it is to you to grab the moments of peacefulness and tranquillity? Don't hear me saying that you can't live in a big city, and that if you do, you need to pack it up and move to a farm in Iowa. My point is that the food for our soul is found in a consistent place of escape from the rush hour traffic and daily to-do lists. I chill out with our friend, Jesus. We've only got a mist of a time table to enjoy on earth, so we should do just that. Detour your daytimers to a place of stillness, above all the hype, and slow the aging process down. Believe you me, New York is a fun place to visit, but residing with my Creator is a spiritual homestead.

GROW! When was the last time you lead a quiet life? What does it take to do this? How married to your daily schedule are you? Do you find time for God?

VALENTINE'S DAY

READY, *"Love is patient, love is kind, is not jealous, does not brag, isn't arrogant, doesn't act unbecomingly; does not seek its own; is not provoked, doesn't take into account a wrong suffered, doesn't rejoice in unrighteousness, but rejoices in truth, bears all things, believes all things, hopes all things, endures all things. Love never fails."* 1 Corinthians 13:4-8

SET, There aren't many typical days lived experiencing the love which is exchanged on *this* day. Cupid starts firing arrows in the direction of our tender hearts moving us to share this day with someone we love. The card shops, flower nurseries, and candy stores make a killing each year on this day. It seems like the collars tighten up around the male sex to first, not forget February 14th, but even more impressive, to try out those creative skills and come up with a day she won't soon forget. I'm no expert on understanding the opposite sex, but I have learned that it's the little things that really matter. You don't have to be married or have a relationship going on to have a sweetheart. It could be that a sister, mom or another female relative falls into the category of a valentine. The cards are cute, the flowers are favorites, and the candy dandy, but Valentine's Day is love God's way.

When you read what Paul wrote to the church in Corinth, he defines what we should be wrapping up in our actions to give to our sweeties. This love is a written description of what God's true love is to you as a child of God. God celebrates this special day year round. Do you know how people would view you, if you really took to heart (pun) these verses in your life daily? Give a gift today that won't wilt without water, that doesn't melt under heat, or end up in a scrapbook. That gift is applied scripture. Look out cupid, this is one arrow that shoots long and deep into our hearts.

GROW! What ways can you show your sweetheart you really value them?

WITH ALL DUE RESPECT

READY, *"Honor your father and mother, that your days may be pro-longed in the land which the Lord gives you." Exodus 20:12*

SET, The United States Code says that "the flag represents a living country and is itself considered a living thing." There is a set of rules which accompany this code: for example, standing at attention and facing the flag with the right hand over the heart. The flag should never touch the ground or be used as wearing apparel. The flag should be displayed during school days and near every polling place on election days. When raising the flag, it should be hoisted quickly and lowered slowly.

I don't know about you, but for the majority of Americans, this stuff seems to be a lost tradition. Most folks don't even know to take off their 'lids' (hats) when putting up or taking down the flag. Why is it that this great nation of ours, you know, the one nation under God, has such a distorted view of our past history? I believe I know...lack of **respect.** The closest that some folks ever come to that word is singing Aretha Franklin's hit, *R-E-S-P-E-C-T* on an old 45 rpm record.

No matter what you might have heard on TV's *20/20* documentaries, we live in a great country. We see public flag-burnings nowadays about as often as we see car wrecks. If we knew, or had a relative who fought and died for this great nation, I think it would be a little burr under our saddle to see Ole Glory go up in a puff of smoke. Why are some irreverent to the flag under which we live? Lack of respect. This same scenario holds true in our society of siblings who disobey and run uncontrollably in our homes and on the streets because of no respect for their parents. Respect is not some title we put on an album, but a responsibility to our authority. God put you with the parents or authority figures in your life for a specific purpose, and you are to obey them under the borders of the Bible. I realize you sometimes wonder if they have a clue as to what they're doing, and the answer is, they are doing the best they can (parenting is tough stuff). Allow them to make mistakes in the process, yet respect and obey them, too. Being both an American citizen and an obedient child are things to be proud of.

GROW! What does respect mean to you? How can you show your parent(s) more respect?

A CHEERFUL GIVER

READY, *"Let each one do just as he has purposed in his heart, not grudgingly or under compulsion; for God loves a cheerful giver." 2 Corinthians 9:7*

SET, There tells a story of a wealthy man who lived in Scotland years ago. He had outlived all of his family and was recently diagnosed with a terminal illness that would allow him only a few months to live. He had been successful in about every business deal he had been involved with and was looked upon by the locals in high esteem. during his final chapter of his life he wanted to know what is was like to live as a beggar on the streets, scurrying for food like a street rat. One day he was digging through a pule of rubbish for a morsel of food when a poor young boy came up to join in the search. After a few minutes the boy, being a pro, found half a loaf of stale bread, and the wealthy man found none. The boy, with excitement of the find, jumped for joy and began to devour the bread. All of a sudden, he noticed the wealthy man (disguised as a beggar) had no food, so he gave him the half loaf and walked away. The man, heart-felt at what had just taken place, ran after the boy to say thanks. He asked the boy, "Why did you give me your only meal this week?" to which the poor boy replied, "To give is to get." The man, amazed at the boy's answer and heart, decided to give him his entire inheritance of wealth.

We live in a 'me first' world where our national motto should be 'looking out for number one' (and that's self). What a joy it is to have the privilege of giving to someone in need. In the story of the widow's mite, you see a great example of not only giving of a mite (last penny), but also giving with a cheerful heart. Giving comes from the heart, not the pocketbook. Giving doesn't necessarily have to be money, it could be a listening ear, service, or time. God loves a joyful giver who's not as concerned with the ten percent tithe issue as He is the attitude in which you give. What a testimony you will be to simply meet someone's need by giving. Who knows, God has His ways of rewarding you far better than you'll ever know from a savings account. Remember, to get, you've got to give it up.

GROW! When was the last time you gave? Who could you give to today? What does Jesus say in His word about giving? (Look it up.)

CRY BABY

READY, *"Then all the people (Israelites) lifted up their voices and cried, and the people wept all night." Numbers 14:1*

SET, I remember learning in a high school health class how good crying is for us. It serves many purposes such as relieving stress, washing out foreign debris from the eye socket, and unclogging the tear ducts of babies and probably adults too. No matter how tough someone may seem, we all have cried at some point or another in our lives. Crying can be a part of a mourning process after the loss of a loved one, or a reaction from lack of sleep, or release of too much stress. Whatever the cause, it is a God-made way of dealing or coping in life.

Moses and Joshua dealt with a different kind of crying as they led a whole mess of people (Israelites) out of slavery, across the desert, and through the Red Sea (sounds like *over the river and through the woods to Grandmother's house we go),* and put up with a whole bunch of whining. The problem didn't stem from pure motives or sincere faith, but the lack of. You see, this is a great example of how not all expressed emotion such as crying and weeping is sincere. At times, people shed tears that are not valid. Some moments, you can see that the tears are of anger or lack of faith (God failed them), and they are *wrong.* Don't take a God-given emotion and use it as a mortal manipulation. You can see in this example that God allowed these people to wander in the wilderness until *all* of them died off, because they were wrong in their ways. Go ahead, cry all you want to, just make sure it's not a fake.

GROW! When was the last time you cried? What caused it? How did you solve the situation that provoked it, or did you? Have you ever cried insincere tears? Why?

70

INTEGRITY

READY, "Is not the fear of God your confidence, and the integrity of your ways your hope?" Job 4:6

SET, If there is one key ingredient missing today in the Christian's secret recipe, it would be *integrity.* We live in a society that is losing its grip on the true check-list of character qualities. One hundred million people watch or listen to religious television and radio broadcasts each day. Winston Churchill stated, "Technology is going faster than morality." You might be asking yourself, "Self, just what does this word mean?" Let me, if you will, define this word in a language you can understand. Integrity is when you are the same person on the inside as you are on the outside. You're the same in a hotel room a thousand miles away from home as you are when you're sitting in church. Integrity is being a person of commitment and being bound by your word. You could say that you walk your talk around your peers and in the private places of your life. Your tongue will not be flapping like a flag in the wind with gossip as your venom. Integrity says that when you say, "I do", that means until death.

Isn't it a relief that when Moses came down from Mt. Sinai, he didn't come down with the Ten Suggestions? Our Christian belief is filled with absolutes with little room for finding loop-holes. Isn't it nice to know that our God doesn't have a bad day and decide to send another flood to destroy every morsel of mankind without warning, even though he promised he wouldn't? My Father and your Father in heaven is bent on maintaining a model of integrity for you and I to follow. You might be asking yourself, since we live in a society where integrity is scarcely found, "How could little ol' me make a difference and begin to change the trend of the 90's?" Does your vote really matter? Yes! With God as your guide, it does matter. One vote put Hitler in a position, one vote brought Texas into the Union...so I guess you do matter after all.

GROW! What will integrity do for your example? How can you show integrity today to others?

READY, "Be still and know that I am God." Psalm 46:10

SET, In this civilization of chaos, living frantically on the fast track, there are few times in our daily schedules we could classify as quiet, still times. Don't you feel like you're the hamster in the cage on a wheel going like mad, and you're on display for others to see? An article in the Boston newspaper tells how after Lenny Bias, first round draft choice of the Boston Celtics, was found dead of an overdose of cocaine, they questioned his high school coach, who said, "It looks like life in the fast lane got even faster." The pace of society doesn't exactly promote or applaud times of stillness and silence. Ever been in a conversation, or with a group of people, when all turned silent?. Man, do the body languages start speaking, as heads start bowing, fingers and toes go to tapping with nervous gestures. Let's face up to it, we don't like quiet or the fact that we're still, because we *feel* like time is passing us by without anything productive happening. Just the opposite is true to God. Be sure you don't let your feelings become fact in this situation.

God, being a Creator of care, doesn't want to try to speak above the volume of society. You and I both know when God needs to get our attention, He can. But He chooses not to, unless we want Him to. Learn, while you're young, to find a consistent quiet time daily, in a specific location, which is like a secret hide-out that only you and the Savior know about. When you're at that spot and begin to read His word, study it. When you pray for guidance, listen to His answer. You can't do all this while on the treadmill of life. Who knows, you may begin to glow after meeting with God each day...Moses did.

GROW! Did you find a still, quiet place today to visit with Jesus? Why not? How can you?

Second Wind

READY, *"Do all your work heartily for the Lord rather than for men." Colossians 3:23*

SET, It was a hot August day, and I happened to be wearing a hot football uniform under the guidance of a hot-tempered coach. These three did not go well for my health during two-a-day workouts preparing for the upcoming season. I remember how that day's practice schedule went about as slow as a duck swimming in oil. It drug on and on and on and finally when what I hallucinated to be the final sound, I heard my coach say, "Boys, everyone on the line for some *pukers.*" Sorry for the graphic language, but that meant we now had to run sprints until we dropped. I felt like this would be the perfect time to get run over by a steam roller, just to extinguish my pain. I was on the line ready to drop when out of the corner of my helmet, between the face guard bars, I saw...beauty in the bleachers. Yep, my girlfriend had come to watch her sugar plum, sweetie pie, honey muffin practice. Hot dog, did I perk up, pooch out my chest, stand up tall, and begin to clap and cheer up my teammates who were ready for a stretcher. It's like a second wind (maybe just puppy love) came over me, and you'd think I'd been shot out of a cannon, the way I ran those sprints. Miracles still happen.

We are a people who are in the *do* mode most of the time. We go, go, go, like a hamster on a treadmill, day in and day out. We work, serve, slave throughout our lives, but for whom? Are we trying to earn our ticket abroad the Heavenly Airways Express? To do *whatever* you're doing for your Creator and not your crowd will take a new perspective, seeing how we live in a performance based acceptance world. God is more than happy to help in this process that starts in a prayer. Give God your glory and see if your reward isn't relished more. Imagine God in the bleachers, cheering you on in your daily tasks and see if you don't find a second wind.

GROW! Do you do all you do for you, or who? What kind of work do you do daily? How can you give the glory to God?

READY, "*And everyone who hears these words of Mine, and doesn't act upon them, will be a foolish man, who built his house upon the sand and the rain and floods came and the winds blew and it beat upon that house and it fell, and great was its fall.*" *Matthew 7:26-27*

SET, If you aren't already, you will someday be involved in of one of the largest investments a person will make in a lifetime...a house. Whether you are going to build, buy or lease, you will sink about one third of your paycheck into this money-muncher. A home is a nest for a family and a refuge from the rat race. You put your money, mind, and muscle into making it your dream home, the kind you imagined while growing up. The style may be Victorian, contemporary, or rustic; it may be spread out, two story, or split level; the colors may be subdued or outstanding. Whatever the case, it will be yours to call 'home, sweet home.' Through the Sermon on the Mount, Jesus gave insights for living. Jesus warns you of what happens to a home (meaning your life) that is built on false pretenses. Jesus reminds us that tough times, like bad weather, will come. As in buying or building a house, you must first check out the foundation's structure to make sure it is built on a firm footing of rock. You build your life each day either on the soft sands of society or the bedrock of Christ. What will it be, a house that stands through the storms of time, or a shack that melts like cardboard at the first sign of bad weather? You're not forced, but you are warned of the consequences of a poorly built home. In today's world we have building inspectors that do the checking for us. In our spiritual life we have fellow believers that warn us of a faulty framework. Heed these warnings not only in your pursuit of the 'Great American Dream,' but also in your journey with Jesus.

GROW! What kind of foundation have you built your life on? Is it on sand or 'the Rock'? If sand, what can you do to beef up the framework?

THE TRAP

READY, "But each one (you) is tempted (trapped) when he is carried away and enticed by his own lust." James 1:14

SET, I'm gonna' tell you a real life happening which is tough to swallow but really brings this verse home, so bear with me. The sport of trapping animals, fish, etc. has been in existence for centuries. There are different reasons for this sport (if you want to call it that), and sometimes it's done humanely for a good reason. All too often, it's done for no positive reason. In this scenario, we're talking of how raccoons are trapped. If you've ever seen one of these creatures in the wild, you notice several character qualities. First, they are clean animals who are required to wash all their food, because they have no saliva glands to assist in the swallowing process. Second, they are very curious, and are always into things and situations they shouldn't be. Third, coons use trees as hiding places, so they're great tree climbers with powerful hind legs. One way a trapper, trapping coons for their fur, would use these qualities against the coon itself, is by covering a small six inch steel trap with leaves and placing it under a three foot branch, hanging from it a piece of shiny metal or foil. Following this set-up, the coon, with its curious nature, would see the shining object, stand up to touch it with its front paws and walk right into the trap. The trap would engage and, with severe force speed-cut the hind legs off the animal and leave it unable to seek shelter in a tree (no back legs). The coon would lie there and bleed to death.

This world, in which you live, is full of soul trappers looking to destroy you with the glamour and glitter of what the world has to offer. You are a curious creature who could be enticed (fishing terminology for lure) to play with what looks good (sex, money, etc.) and end up snared by the trap of Satan. If you think the story which was told is mean, you have a similar scenario going on around you every second you live. Folks who play get badly burned and some are never able to recover. Don't be easily deceived, and know that the world will offer you something which appears good to rob you of something great (God's gift). You see, Satan knows our weaknesses and uses them to destroy us.

GROW! What does the world offer you that glitters? How can you steer clear of the trap?

SAME OL' SAME OL'

READY, *"Jesus Christ is the same yesterday and today and forever."*
Hebrews 13:8

SET, Have you ever woke with what I call "the same ol' blues"?
You know what I'm talking about...when you wake up to that same
ol' alarm clock, walk into the same ol' bathroom, look into that
same ol' mirror, see that same ol' rack-head, use that same ol'
toothbrush, look into that same ol' closet at those same ol' tired,
out of style clothes, crack your shins on that same ol' table on your
way to that same ol' kitchen to eat that same ol' cereal in that same
ol' bowl and head off to that same ol' school to do that same ol'
study stuff, come home to do that same ol' homework, go to sleep
in that same ol' bed just to wake up and do that same ol' thing
again the next day! (Okay, it's over.)

We are geared this age to want change, the newest, coolest
ways and things. I mean, come on, you buy a new outfit, pair of
Nikes, computer, or car, and in a matter of days it's outdated and
obsolete. It's tough to keep up the ol' image and even tougher on
the pocket book to keep up with styles. There is a boat we are
missing on this trip of life called *traditions, anchors, dependability,
and assurance.* What if God decided to change His ways mid-
stream? What if the Ten Commandments changed as often as shoe
styles? What if Jesus decided to return to earth in a flash telling us
the 'Heaven deal' is off? We have a great deal of hope *knowing* (not
wondering) that Jesus and His standards never have, nor ever will
change. Jesus Christ is exactly the same today as two thousand
years ago, and will be the same in another two thousand years (if
we last that long). Take refuge in this incredibly stable thought in
the midst of very turbulent worldly waves. Sometimes the same ol'
same ol' ain't half bad.

GROW! How would you feel if Jesus changed His ways weekly?
Isn't it comforting to know beyond a shadow of a doubt that your
Savior is a tradition? Are you happy now? Why?

EARTH SUITS

READY, *"Do you not know that your body is a temple of the Holy Spirit who is in you, whom you have from God, and that you are not your own?" 1 Corinthians 6:19*

SET, Today's devo is a subject that we all live with and yet can't seem to ever be satisfied with. What subject might that be? Your ol' *bod.* Only today, we will classify and rename this concentrated mass of skin and bones as an *Earth Suit.* Do you realize the amount of money spent on marketing and advertising products designed with the sole purpose to better that bag of bones? Hours sweated upon hours are spent daily, running, walking, lifting, playing, biking, rowing, skiing, swimming, climbing, and dying in our society each day. Don't read me wrong and think for a minute that I don't condone these frolicking physical activities, because I do. What happens in our society is a philosophy of thinking that if 'something is worth doing, it's worth *over*doing.' The challenge is to stay trim and fit for the righteous reasons, and not the worldly whims. The issue is not one of priorities, but one of perspective. In a social atmosphere which puts emphasis on the outward lookers, over the inward beauties, we need to beware. Our value order needs to first be to develop those God fashioned, inward character qualities, and then begin to focus on the outward temple.

Years ago I asked a seventy-two year old man, who exercised religiously five days a week his entire life and looked to be the picture of a physical specimen, how he could stay so consistent in his training. His answer was simple, yet truthful, "I don't want Jesus to live in a run down house." Wow! How true that we are where Jesus resides and calls home. How those simple words can give us a proper perspective and purpose for keeping fit and trim, rather than our motive being to look like a model on the cover of a magazine, or to have muscles to bulge out at the ladies. If you're already working out, stay with it. If not, get after it...but do it for the right reasons. Now go on, lift those weights, climb those stairs, swim those laps, run those miles, bike those trails, play those sports, and *Just Do It for Jesus.*

GROW! Do you see your body as a dwelling place of your Savior? How can you maintain a balanced life? Why should you start today to remodel your home (body)?

77

THE STEALTH BOMBER

READY, "*The thief comes to kill and destroy, but I have come that you might have life, and have it more abundantly.*" *John 10:10*

SET, I don't think we will ever forget the night we heard, broadcast live by President Bush, that we had launched our first air-strike and started our ground troops in motion in the war called Desert Storm. One could hardly even watch a commercial or listen to a song on the radio entirely without an interrupting update on the war. I recall the unleashing and mystical use of a new age of technology assault plane called the Stealth Bomber. It had advance components, flew at great speeds undetectable by enemy radar, carried big bombs and looked like a black bat out of some video game. Its purpose was to be able to steal into enemy territory unobserved, surprise attack, and return to its base without a peep. Maybe a better name could have been the 'Deceiving Destructor.'

Realize it or not, we as Christians are in a spiritual war every day of our waking lives. We too, are being confronted with an enemy who is unseen and unpredictable by the naked eye. Our enemy attacks not to take survivors, but shoots to kill and destroy, taking no prisoners. How real do you think Satan is? How much time do you take each day to prepare yourself to do battle with the dark side of life? The Stealth is no different than the fallen angel, yet we continue to let down our guard and go into battle unprepared to win. Yes, we have won the war at the cross on Calvary with a single soldier, Jesus, yet a constant battle for our hearts and minds is being fought. Don't be deceived by the silence or the lack of visual evidence, because the enemy lurks in the darkness. Believe you me, when he attacks, only the faithful find freedom. Stand firm, put on your armor daily, and realize you have all the weapons you need to stay standing...His promise and His word.

GROW! When was the last time you had a sneak attack catch you off guard? How can you prepare to prevent another one? How sweet is a victory in Christ?

READY, *"But let each one of us examine his own work, and then he will have reason for boasting in regard to himself alone, and not in regard to one another." Galatians 6:4*

SET, Consistently throughout my growing up days and even at times now, I struggle with comparing myself to others. I would compare myself athletically, anatomically, monetarily, intellectually, behaviorally, and structurally. The results of this continual contrast of myself to another world were inward stress, dishonesty, discontentment, hopelessness, and an overall crudy self-image. I'm happy to say, I'm not alone in this tornado of try-to-be's. We have a culture full of murderers, folks committing suicide, stealing, depressed, and using drugs and alcohol to ease the pain of not quite ever matching up.

When I was a kid I recall my dad telling me one very important inside secret to learning to ride a bike... "Don't look to the right or left, just keep looking straight ahead." God tells Joshua the same bit of advice when he is wondering how in the heck he's gonna' lead three million people into the promised land. The apostle Paul tells us to 'fix our eyes on Jesus,' but not on ourselves or others.

In Antarctica the people deal with not only the harsh elements, but also wild animals. The wolf is at times a terrible problem and threat to their safety. The way they killed these animals was not to hunt and shoot them but to dip a large sharp knife in blood, stick it handle first in the snow and let the blood freeze on the sharp blade. The wolves smelled the blood, began to work themselves into a frenzy, licking the knife, and, therefore, cut their own tongues to pieces while bleeding to death.

Now, I know that story is a little tough to stomach, but so are people who compare themselves into a frantic state and begin to lick on the edge of worldliness. Don't compare yourself to anyone but the Savior. Don't live a life of matching up. Don't lick yourself to death...it's just not worth it.

GROW! In what ways do you compare yourself? Do you ever match up? What happens when you compare to the standard of Christ?

That Line Is Busy...Wanna' Hold?

READY, "*I love the Lord because He hears my voice (prayers) and my supplications.*" Psalm 116:1

SET, In this age of communication headaches and technological takeovers, you almost don't know which lie to believe. AT&T is slamming MCI, and MCI is mocking US Sprint, and US Sprint is manipulating AT&T...when will this cycle stop? No matter how advanced our phone lines become, we will always be one step behind the population growth of this county. In other words, by the time you expand and get up to date you are already one step behind. We have fancy little gadgets and gimmicks like call waiting, party-lines, conference lines, voice mail, and call forwarding, but no solutions to the age old problem of busy signals. Where I work the phone seems to ring off the hook all day long, but I've realized I can only talk on one line at a time. Therefore, someone is *always* on hold, waiting. Isn't it a bummer when you call someone long distance or from a pay phone and you're put on hold for an hour or cut off for some unknown reason? How do you feel when you're put through to the wrong extension and you talk ten minutes to the wrong person before you realize he is not who you thought it was? Oops!

Here are some words of hope for your listening ears...God puts *no one* on hold. AT&T should have God as a consultant to their technology department, because He is always one step ahead of the game. What if...when you had an important or maybe life threatening request for the Creator and all you got was an angelic operator message singing, "That line is busy...would you like to call back?" Or how about, if in a moment of sorrow or pain, you cry out to the Lord and all of a sudden you heard a dial tone because you got cut off? Gnarly, dude! You can take this and deposit in a bank...God cares for you and values His time to communicate with you through the phone lines of prayer. So, while the 'Big Three' are battling out who is the cheapest long distance carrier...remember, Jesus paid your phone bill on the cross, so talk all you want.

GROW! What do you feel like when you're put on hold? What about hung up on? How does it make you feel to know that God puts no one on hold? Call Him today!

FESS UP

READY, *"Then the King said to him, 'How many times must I tell you to speak to me nothing but the truth in the name of the Lord?'"* 2 Chronicles 18:15

SET, One of the favorite pastimes at our ranch while growing up was to shoot water moccasin snakes in our pond. They were a hazard to our bullfrog population, not to mention they could bite the fire out of ya.' These slithery, slimy, scum surviving snakes were best seen sunning on the shore on a hot summer's day (say that sentence fast ten times). We would drive our tractor to the edge of the bank, raise up the bucket full of friends, guns, and plenty of ammo to its full extension for maximum viewing, then commence to firing away at will. One day, our routine snake hunt turned into an unplanned nightmare. We accidentally drove the forty thousand dollar tractor into the pond. Man, oh man, did I know that I was gonna get it. My dad wasn't with us; in fact no parent was, and we all knew if he found out we would all hang at high noon. We got a neighboring farmer to pull out the submerged submarine, cleaned it up, raked the tire tracks leading into the pond, and got it running again by 2:00 a.m.

How many times have you been in a pure pickle that you knew would spell out pure trouble? The real question is, did you ever get away with it scot-free? Did you lie or just not tell at all? How characteristic that in story after story we see biblical characters doing the same? You know, hey...what they don't know can't hurt them, or one white lie never killed anyone. The problem comes when we start small, and it becomes a common routine in our lives. God, whether you know it or will admit it, is everywhere at once and is all knowing. He sees deceit, cheating, lying, stealing, hating, and defiling even when common folks don't. He is faithful and just to forgive us of these, yet we are called also to make it right with the person(s) we victimized. Keeping a clean slate is tough, yet our conscience is relieved when we do. I know you're wondering what I did. Yes, I did conceal the truth, and yes, my dad did find out. How?...(suspense is building isn't it?) the neighbor told him and yes, I did get it!

GROW! When was the last time you lied? Did you confess or conceal? How will you handle if differently next time?

A GIANT SUCCESS

READY, *"What will be done for the man (giant) who kills this Philistine and takes away the reproach from Israel? Who is this that he should taunt the armies of the living God?" 1 Samuel 17:26*

SET, You have probably read this or had it read to you at bedtime or maybe even in Sunday school class. Remember it? It's the one about an overlooked young man named David and an ugly giant named Goliath, who had a little disagreement on issues, so they went head to head. David had an ancient sling-shot and rocks as his artillery, and Goliath, a big sword that could have been used as a double for an airplane wing. David was on paper, outsized, out-muscled, out equipped, and should be considered out-to-lunch for even taking on this dude. Well, enough, you know how this story goes, David smacks this giant in the coconut with a rock and hence becomes the King of Israel (Cliff Notes version). What David gave us in this bit of scripture is more than a fun bedtime story, it's the secret to success when facing overwhelming odds in our lives. Check out these six secrets to success: 1) David sized himself up before he sized up the obstacle. Note: Ignorance about yourself is a self imposed obstacle. 2) Don't let the failure of others stop you. Note: Most failures are followed by successes. 3) Former victories will guide future successes. Note: Nothing breeds success like success. 4) Don't be handcuffed by traditional thinking. Note: Be aware of statements like "we've always done it that way before." What works for others may not work for you. 5) You will have to find courage to stand alone at times. Note: God will never leave or forsake you. 6) Never forget who gives you success. Note: God alone gives success.

Look around you and see all the folks who strive a lifetime to gain success. Success itself is not wrong, as long as one is striving for the right reasons. The process too, is part of the beauty that God allows you to enjoy during your journey. Go ahead...take on the Goliath in your life with the weapon God provides, His Word and your knees.

GROW! What is a major challenge (Giant) you face today? Are you equipped for the battle? Is God behind you?

READY, "Realize this, in the last days, difficult times will come. For men will become lovers of self, money, boastful, arrogant, disobedient to parents, ungrateful, unholy, unloving, gossips, brutal, haters of good, conceited, lovers of pleasure rather than lovers of God; holding to a form of godliness although they have denied its power, avoid such men as those." 2 Timothy 3:2-5

SET, For years I thought that this verse was aimed at communicating the details of a fallen world headed for Hell in a hand basket. It seems to give the specifics of what this society will be looking like prior to the return of the Creator. Guess what? There are two ways to look at something...my way and the right way. It just so happens that Paul is describing what the Church is going to look like with all its splendor in the last days. Don't hang up on me yet and mishear what I'm saying. I *am* an avid church member and a firm believer in the body of Christ meeting weekly. I'm not big on giant steeples, ornate pews, and lofty budgets being our only definition of a church, but I do believe the Church is the bride of Christ. Take a moment to read this scripture again...slowly.

Beware of a church and a teacher (pastor or priest) who don't preach the truth and live it out in their own lives. Heed the warnings Paul gives Timothy in these verses of validity: there *will be* churches that are not what God intended them to be. How do you know if a church is for real? What sort of check-list can be used to test its spiritual substance? A legitimate church 1) *takes God and the Bible seriously,* believes it is the inerrant word, teaches about Jesus' deity, servanthood, humility, faith, purity, creation, agape love, discipleship, Heaven and Hell, and doesn't water down or misuse scripture, 2) *looks hard at what God has wrapped up in you;* has some expectations of you and how your unique contributions can be better used in the body of Christ; helps you to realize your importance in the family, 3) *is an equipping church;* provides its congregation with tools to live; pastoral staff sees itself as a coaching staff; equips you to do the work of the ministry. Once you've found a church that qualifies, pour not only your heart into it, but your actions too...it's well worth the effort.

GROW! What should a Godly church look and act like? Do a check-list on your church...how does it come out?

A Weak Think

READY, *"For as he thinks within himself, so he is." Proverbs 23:7*

SET, Years ago I went along with a handful of fellow believers on a mission trip to Trinidad. Now, hear me out, I couldn't even spell it, much less feel spiritual enough to do such a trip -but I went anyway. To give you a run down of this Third World country is a sad story. Dirt poor, used and abused by the oil industry, no stable government in place, apathy running rampant, immorality evident, and directions to nowhere. Our mission was to go door to door to every house on the island and personally share Jesus with a population whose religious melting pot included Hindus, Muslims, and a few Rastifarians for flavor. While sharing with a gas station attendant for about thirty minutes, I looked over the register counter to see a sign that read, "The brain is only as strong as its weakest think." What a fact of scriptural truth, yet a catchy play on the original, "the chain is only as strong as its weakest link."

If you think for a moment you'll realize all it took for adultery, murder, theft, gossip, lying, disobedience, rebellion, lust, greed, envy, and a long, long list was a weak think moment. What's that? That is a time when you weren't in tune with God and you followed the old nature path. It's the second you gave up hope for harmony, purity for passion, or contentment for compromise. Realize that you *are* gonna' have those weak moments, you will lose a few battles (you're saved, not perfect), but you don't have to lose the war. We are overcomers!

GROW! When was the last 'weak think' moment you had? How can you avoid it next time? What prevents those moments in your life?

A REAL PEDICURE

READY, "*If then, the Lord and the Teacher, washed your feet, you also ought to wash one another's feet.*" *John 13:14*

SET, It should have been His time to recline, kick up His feet, and say, "Serve Me." He was the one who was fixin' to hang on a cross upon the city dump pile and die for a cause, not them. The disciples should have been looking for every opportunity to show their appreciation and love to Him. It was His last supper, not theirs. It was His hour to wave the banner and sign the autographs, not theirs. But as usual, God's way is not our way. Even though in ancient times, the teacher with the higher rank was to sit at the head of the table and the rookie was to do the dirty grunt labor. It is always amazing to see just what servanthood, true serving, looks like in full swing. Jesus, looking for every opportunity to use a teachable moment with His running buddies (disciples) seized the moment and grabbed the towel and wash bowl first. I'm sure there wasn't exactly a rush, nor did any disciple pull a hamstring to get to do this lovely job of washing all those nasty feet. This janitorial job was one for the low ranking, not the top brass.

One of the key ingredients to the special recipe of Christianity is serving. To be a Christ-like servant you must first be humble in spirit. Second, you must be willing (we're all able) and thirdly, have a watchful eye for opportunity. You wanna' make a grand appearance or leave your mark on this world? Do you want to go out in a blaze of glory? Then serve someone else. Washing feet was for the maid of the house, not the owner of the world. You have and will have, today a chance to humble yourself and serve someone if you only look for the chance (they come often). If you're feeling sorry for yourself, down or depressed, don't take an aspirin, just serve someone else. Serving has a way of taking your eyes off self and putting them on else.

GROW! When was the last time you served someone? Have you ever washed someone else's feet (literally) like your parents, friend, etc.? Who can you serve today? Are you following our Lord Jesus' example in serving?

JESUS #3?

READY, *"But I say to you who hear, love your enemies and pray for those who persecute you." Matthew 5:44*

SET, A few years back I was waiting in a friend's living room before going out to dinner and noticed a very interesting title on the book shelf. I know curiosity killed the cat, but I ain't no cat, so I went over and picked it up. The book was *100 of the Most Influential People in the World.* As I browsed through it I quickly noticed that Jesus was ranked number three behind Isaac Newton and Mohammed (not the fighter either). Man, was I as mad as a chained guard dog! I could not believe this flaky author had the guts or lack of brains to put Jesus behind those boneheads. What was he thinking (he must not have been)? Then at the end of the chapter on Jesus, I read where the author literally apologized for not putting Him as number one, citing several reasons. He stated Jesus could not be ranked before the others because Jesus' believers don't obey His words. Quoting Matthew 5:44, the author explained that he had seen few Christians praying for the folks who persecuted them, or loving their enemies. He stated that the followers of Mohammed did as they were commanded and therefore deserved recognition. Wow, what a blow! Here we are again—Christians with egg on our faces!

Gang, we as followers, ambassadors, disciples, or believers have to be obedient to our Master's ways. Yes, the author probably wasn't a believer, but he called it like he saw it, which is his and every other non-Christian's right. You see, we live our lives under a microscope, like it or not. No, we are not perfect, just forgiven, and we have to change our ways if we actually want to be a light and make a difference. Begin today to give it all you can to obey and trust in the final outcome. The results could be, who knows...maybe a number one ranking in that guy's book for Jesus someday. Miracles can happen.

GROW! Do you obey God's word? What percentage of the time? Why do you sometimes not? Do you think Jesus should have been number one? What can **you** do to get Him there in this world's eyes?

PARTICIPANT OR SPECTATOR

READY, *"Do you not know that those who run in a race all run, but only one receives the prize? Run in such a way that you might win." 1 Corinthians 9:24*

SET, Several years ago, I decided (I must have fallen on my head) that I would begin to train for a 10K road race. Boy, did I get sick of pounding the pavement like a parade of polar bears day in and day out. I trained about three months, running my longest times on the weekends to prepare for this event. I made a phone call to a buddy in Dallas and asked him to sign me up in one of those races I'd seen on ESPN with the live band at the finish line, free tee-shirts, food, and lots of enthusiastic bystanders to cheer me on. Little did I know, until I arrived at the race site early one Saturday morning, that I had enlisted in a Pro-Am cross-country championship being held in the area. Six point two miles up and down, over and through obstacles, against a stacked field of fifty of the top runners in the world (some four minute milers). Now, it didn't take me long (my wife helped clue me in) to see that this would be a rough first outing. When I finally finished, the awards ceremony was over, the band didn't exist, and I had come in fifty-second place (a dog beat me too).

I learned a valuable lesson that I won't soon forget. First of all, never trust a friend to sign you up in a road race, and second, no matter where you race or how tough it is, the finish line is still worth going for. As believers in Christ, we all need to be focused on the hope of Heaven at the end of this Christian race. Many are entering the race, but not enough are participating and running to their fullest potential. By the time the race has started, the participants have changed clothes and are now spectators. Be a righteous runner for God, having faith that there is a finish line in Heaven.

Everyone can run a hundred yard dash with no training whatsoever (it may take a calendar year), yet we are called to run a marathon which requires daily training in the Word. Don't be afraid to enter. God takes care of the details; all He calls you to do is run. On your mark, get set...**go!**

GROW! Are you a spectator or a participant? What motivates you to run?

READY, *"A joyful heart is good medicine, but a broken spirit dries up the bones." Proverbs 17:22*

SET, The *Executive Digest* printed an interesting article on the results of a scientific study of the effect of laughter on humans. The study showed that laughter had a profound effect on virtually every important organ in our bodies. The study showed that laughter reduced tension and relaxed the tissues as well as exercising them. It said that even when laughter was forced it resulted in beneficial effects, both mentally and physically. So the next time you feel nervous or stressed out, or have the jitters, indulge in a good gut laugh and see what happens.

Laughter, when untainted, can be one of the most productive resources known to mankind. It is amazing how in the midst of this rough and tumble world, when laughter makes an appearance, it soothes our souls. Laughter was invented by God and was intended to be used for a kind of spiritual medicine. Have you ever noticed that laughter produces smiles, and smiles seem to be contagious? Joy seems to be born from the capability to laugh in the midst of trials (pain). Learning to laugh at yourself and not take yourself too seriously is a benefit in itself. Warning: don't be of the type that chimes in with the distasteful or discolored (ungodly) humor that you find around a lot. When you're having a gut buster of a chuckle, make sure its stimulus is pure and holy in the sight of the Savior. Once again, Satan has taken a God-made product and distorted its true purpose. Go ahead, laugh at something goofy you or a friend did (be careful not to demean), laugh at a 'foot in mouth' incident, or a hilarious situation. You'll be amazed at just how healing this medicine can be and you don't need a doctor's prescription to use it.

GROW! What are the benefits that you see in laughter? When did you last have a gut wrenching laugh? How did it make you feel? What makes you laugh? Would Jesus laugh with you?

Our God Is An Awesome God

READY, *"Then he said, 'I am the God of your father, the God of Abraham, the God of Isaac, and the God of Jacob.' At this, Moses hid his face, because he was afraid to look at God." Exodus 3:6*

SET, You know the true spiritual giants who exist today are those few who at some time become realistically conscious of the real presence of God and maintain that consciousness throughout their daily lives. A sincere Christian experience must always include a genuine encounter with the Creator. Without this, a personal relationship is a mere reflection of reality and a cheap copy of the original. This is when the "visible image of the invisible God" (Colossians 1:15) appears to be a religious ritual instead of an intimate relationship.

Your encounter could be that of terror like Abraham's "thick and dreadful darkness" (Genesis 15:12), or as when Moses had to hide his face, because he was afraid. Usually this fear will turn to awe and level off at a reverent sense of closeness. We know those saints of past weren't perfect, but they walked in conscious communion with the real presence of God. When they prayed, they did so as if they were speaking to someone who actually existed. The essential point is, these were men who experienced God.

I know you're probably wondering if I am a few bricks shy of a full load. When I refer to an 'experience with God' I am referring to those times when it's just you and God working through a situation. It's like those times when you've obtained a real peace surpassing all worldly understanding, which tells you to go on a mission trip for spring break instead of hanging with your friends in Florida. Catch my drift? To actually walk into the omnipresent, holy quarters of God is an awesome experience. To drop to your knees at bed-time and pray for a miracle or wisdom is awesome. To step out on faith in an area like finances, marriage, or career, and lean totally on divine intervention is awesome. Face it...God is awesome in the truest sense of the word.

GROW! When was the last time you experienced God? In what ways have you ever experienced the presence of God? Were you afraid?

READY, *"Keep watching and praying that you may not enter into temptation, the spirit is willing but the flesh is weak." Matthew 26:41*

SET, It's not like the subject we're gonna' talk about today is new to the scene. You'll find it from the beginning in the garden of Eden to our modern world today. We didn't just recently invent this hazardous material. Archeologists didn't just dig it up. It's *temptation.* Have you ever noticed that we didn't have to be taught to do evil...it comes quite naturally? If you don't believe me, just go hang out at a kindergarten class for an hour or so and watch how little kids (even infants) will very often choose the wrong way. Things don't change too much when it comes to disobedience, they just get a little more sophisticated as we get older. Did you know the Greek meaning of the word obedient is 'to listen'? Basically, we are born with a rebellious spirit sin nature and we seem to like its style at times.

Temptation is a very serious thing, even more so than health insurance and environmental issues. Scripture throughout warns us of its evil venom and painfully far reaching striking distance. The big problem comes when we get into a habit of 'giving in' to its lures of luxury (we think). Temptation is a bridge we cross each day of our lives when we decide between our way or God's. Temptation takes no prisoners and plays no favorites. Temptation scars our hearts, minds, and hardens our conscience. In fact, you could compare this beast to a tactical unit in the military whose sole purpose is to find the weakness in the enemy's army and destroy them. Satan knows what your likes and dislikes are and therefore will attack you at your weak points and moments. This verse gives you ways to overcome these potholes in your path through life. First, remain alert to the enemies sly strategies, second, develop callused knees by praying often, and third, realize that if you rely on your *own* strength you'll end up snake-bit in the end. Watch out...temptation hides in odd places and strikes at unknown times.

GROW! What temptation are you most likely to give in to? What ways do you fight the beast of temptation? If you were Satan how would *you* destroy you? What does the venom of sin carry with it?

FISHIN' HOLE

READY, *"And Jesus said to them, 'Follow me, and I will make you fishers of men' (women too)." Mark 1:17*

SET, Before we begin, let me address you, ladies, before you turn this devo off like a bad TV show. Please, (okay, pretty please with sugar on top) listen up, because this verse applies to you as much as it does the guys. Have you ever been fishin,' either on a lake, river, pond or ocean before? Well, if the answer is yes, then you will relate like an ol' relative. If not, maybe this will motivate you to try it.

Realize this first, that I grew up hunting, but never fishing, so I am definitely no Jimmy Houston (a Pro fisherman). I have done little in life that is as much fun to do with the whole family as landing a 'lunker.' We live close to a great trout lake and try to go as often as we can with the kids on weekends. There is nothing more exciting for a youngster than when the end of the pole takes a dip and begins to tug. Boy howdy, the kid's eyes light up as big as a Texas sunset, and the voice volume begins to go up at the expectation of catching a 'Big One.' Just the thought and anticipation of going to set the line will be enough, even if nothing is caught, to make a fishing outing a success.

I love the way that we can relate today with what happened yesterday in scripture. What would this world be like if we got as excited about 'fishing for friends' as we do about 'landing a lunker'? Notice that you don't have to be qualified to fish. God does that for you, and He *will* make you an angler for people's souls. Again, what a huge deal it is when God depends on *you* to follow Him, and in return you will catch others before they are caught by the evil one. Another important thing, is that Satan always kills his catch, but God chooses the 'catch and release' program. That release is called our freedom in Christ, something not many fine-finned fish can hope for.

GROW! What pond are you fishin' in? What does your spiritual bait look like? Catchin' any?

A Learned Trait

READY, "*For I have learned to be content in all circumstances.*"
Philippians 4:11

SET, One of the hottest behind the counter drugs that Americans use today to cope is Valium. It's kind of a mind tranquilizer that allows oneself to have the attitude of 'let well enough alone.' Call it what you want, take your pick of adjectives like complacent, peaceful, satisfied, at ease, sans souci, not particular, resigned, unaffected, serene, unmolested, comfortable (tired yet?), or unperturbed (whatever). We have a tendency in our terrain to always be wanting on the other side of the fence. The reason that we pop Valium in our diet is the pressure to escape our present situation. Why is it that we're always looking for something better like the newest car, computer, job, house, lingo, style of clothes, hairstyle, or spouse? What happened to loyalty and contentment with where we are at the moment? No, I'm not saying that we are not to strive for perfection or push ourselves, but come on...we've lost that balance. When it begins to be like a game of *Monopoly* where you're continually trying to get more and more, then there is a problem. The apostle Paul speaks louder than a tornado siren when he (of all people) states that he has become content in *all* things. I mean, this guy hasn't had much to brag about to his neighbors in a while. He has been beaten, blamed, and posted bail for being a disciple of Jesus for years. His home has been a jail cell, his life persecuted and his body beaten to a pulp, and *he* says *he* is content no matter if he's in the club house or outhouse. We can learn a huge lesson in life...if we learn to be content in whatever circumstances our sovereign God has placed us in. You know, if we could learn this lesson in God's classroom we wouldn't need the school nurse for aspirin (or Valium) near as much. Then our local drug stores could be selling more cold medicine than pain pills.

GROW! What always makes you want to retreat from a situation? What exactly is contentment? How can you obtain more of it? Is contentment a way of thinking or a place we all come to?

READY, "Blessed is the man who doesn't walk in the counsel of the wicked, stand in the way of sinners or sit in the seat of mockers." Psalm 1:1

SET, You live in a civilization where the majority has ruled throughout history. The greatest injustices of history have been unchecked 'majority rule.' It was the majority that crucified Christ, burned Christians at the stake, established slavery in the South, chuckled when Columbus said the world was round, cut off the ears of John Pym because he advocated the liberty of the press, put Hitler into power, and overturned Roe vs. Wade to legalize abortion. As you can see (and I'm sure could add a lot more to this list), the majority is not necessarily always best for you or your country.

As a Christian you have the governing authority to choose what is right or wrong, to decide to run with the majority and not with the minority. People in our culture (including Christians) have a natural tendency to always choose the easy way. The problem comes when the easy way isn't the right way. You didn't see Jesus choosing to easy way, did you? You didn't hear him saying, "Hey, these spikes in my wrists and this thorn crown on my head are a pain, so I quit." Jesus, the ultimate role model, shows and proves that most of the time the harder way (less traveled) is the best way. Every day you face the intersection of choosing to go with the flow or swim against the current (like a salmon). It's usually the majority that will be drinking, getting divorced, cheating on tests, not telling the truth, or trying pre-marital sex. I'm definitely not telling you this way will be easy, but neither did Jesus. You'll have to have the faith, which is what it takes to stand your ground and do what Jesus would do in every situation and circumstance. Most of the time it's what the few do that leave a lasting impact on the world for Christ.

GROW! Why do most vote with the majority? How tough is it for you to go against the flow? Will you do it today? Why or why not? What kind of impact will you have for standing firm in your faith?

TRAGEDY

READY, "So Delilah said to Samson, 'Tell me the secret of your great strength and how you can be subdued.'" Judges 16:6

SET, A Greek philosopher named Aristotle would have loved the story of Samson and Delilah. The reason is because it would fit his definition of tragedy; to see a strong human be destroyed by a single character flaw. He also claimed that to see this happen should deeply affect those watching. He said that tragedy would lead to a 'catharsis' (cleansing) in those who truly understood what went on. In this gold nugget of scripture one can see that Samson takes a fall. Delilah's Philistine friends have a plot and offer her big bucks to try and chain down the guy who was a symbol of strength to the Israelites. If she could get him to tell the source of his strength she would be well rewarded. Samson may have had bulging muscles but not the brains of his father. Four times Delilah tried (nagged) to subdue Samson before she finally succeeded (you'd think he'd have clued in). Man, oh man, if I was Samson, I'd have chunked this chick out on her head, but he didn't. Why? *Pride!*

Aristotle states that one flaw which gets more folks in trouble is pride. Samson's tragic fall led to the end of his freedom. He became a prisoner and was used as entertainment for the crowds like the headliner of a freak show.

After reading (seeing) a story such as this, we should all learn from someone else's mistake and cleanse ourselves of any pride we might have. We should see ourselves as Samson, committing a grave mistake and falling. This is the scripture we should recall when we catch ourselves walking around all 'puffed up' with pride over some accomplishment, taking credit for it instead of giving the glory to God. Pride is definitely a character flaw which seems to entangle each one of us daily. Say no to the Delilah's of your life who try to get you to sign your autograph or read your own press clippings. Remember, pride goes before a fall.

GROW! What are you most proud about? Who gets the credit when you are successful? How can we be less prideful and more humble?

Two Is Better Than One

READY, *"If one can overpower him who is alone, two can resist him and three strands cannot be quickly torn apart." Ecclesiastes 4:12*

SET, One of the new crazes of our outdoor minded culture is rappelling and rock climbing. I'm sure you've seen breath-taking, heart-stopping pictures of someone on a mountainside, fifteen thousand feet above the forest canopy. One thing you will notice is that the climbers and rappellers always have (unless they're some kinda' nut) a rope as a safety device. Rope, used in this arena, is a combination of a bungee cord and a static line. If you've ever cut through a climbing rope, you know you need a sharp knife and a lot of patience. Why? Because a climbing rope is nothing but a whole bunch of tiny cords or strands all interwoven to form one strong rope. The existence of multi-strands in itself is a security against a rock or sharp object cutting through while one dangles off the side of some cliff.

I love the way we can dive into scripture and discover how these word pictures come alive when exposed. In this specific verse Solomon is identifying the dangerous cliff called Satan we must all climb up throughout our Christian expedition. Satan, wimp that he is, loves to pick on the loner of the herd. Solomon's wisdom is so useful, because Satan can't attack as easily a multitude of believers as he can a lonesome dove. He is basically saying that the more the merrier in this case. On your upward climb to Heaven, you need the security of other saints in the family. Get involved with a body of believers on a weekly agenda. Don't try to climb alone, your rope won't hold and that's when you fall to temptation.

GROW! What sort of fellowship group are you involved in once a week? Why is it so important for you to have other believers as climbing buddies? Do you see the importance of three strand rope?

READY, "When the Chief Shepherd appears, you will receive the unfaded crown of glory." 1 Peter 5:4

SET, You probably have a wall decorated with ribbons, trophies, medals, plaques, letters of recommendations, and awards for a job well done and a goal accomplished. I grew up with a father who was the quarterback of the football team with the longest winning streak (Oklahoma University 1954-58) in the history of the NCAA...forty-seven wins and only one loss. Can you imagine playing four full seasons at anything and only losing one time? Wow, now that is something to pooch your chest and strut around town about. That is an accomplishment that few will ever know and deserves the right to brag You know what? You can go up in my dad's attic, under piles of junk and dust and find all his championship trophies, national championship rings, and plaques. He never displayed them, flaunted or boasted about them; he just didn't see the purpose. His humility and perspective was something you won't see much anymore. A lot of times our self images are all we're wrapped up in.

God calls you to arenas to participate in other events while you're here on earth. This game lasts a lot longer and requires stricter training in order to win His trophies...*crowns.* The difference between earthly and heavenly rewards is that one fades and is forgotten, the other sparkles and survives. The rewards given by God to you for enduring hardship, surviving servanthood and conquering compromise is far greater than any medal, trophy, or plaque. No, those rewards aren't wrong or bad, but they are second place in this category. If you're gonna boast or show off a reward...try a crown from the Creator.

GROW! What honor have you been most proud of that you received? Have you ever been rewarded by God? How? How do they compare eternally?

READY, "*And also that every man should eat and drink, and enjoy the good of all his labor, it is the gift of God.*" *Ecclesiastes 3:13*

SET, Take a moment, rock back in your chair, and ponder (ponder, not take a snooze). Now ask yourself a few direct questions about what you love to do? What do you talk about most? If money was no object, what would you be doing today? What do you do best? After answering those, realize that the joy of your life is determined by doing what you have a piercing passion for doing. Look at the life of Jesus and see His passion every day He roamed the earth. He loved to tango with the tax collectors, fellowship with the fishermen, dialog with the doctors, philosophize with the Pharisees, and commune with the common folk. I dare to doubt that everyday He woke up before His alarm went off, excited about another day of focusing in on His goal and purpose in life. He knew what His mission was, and that it seemed impossible to a faithless world. He held true to His commitment to a lost people, because He knew that failed focus is a reason why so many men fail. There are folks who have taken a job because it's convenient or close to home, yet they are miserable. A friend of mine who is a pastor in Chicago told me one time, "There is nothing more dangerous than being comfortable out of God's will." How true that is with so many folks who have fallen into that hopeless hole. What you love to do is a clue to your calling in life. Jesus knew this and was determined to set the stage for a spectacular climax to thirty three years of being obedient to His calling. Do what makes you happy as long as it is within the parameters of scripture. Live out your dreams with Christ close beside you, after all, dreams are what make this world go around.

GROW! What makes you tick loudest? How are you preparing yourself today for what God has in store for you tomorrow?

RE-RUNS

READY, *"As far as the east is from the west, so far has God thrown away our sins from us." Psalm 103:12*

SET, They're back! What's back? Old re-runs (and they're great)! *The Andy Griffith Show, Flipper, Superman* (black and white version), *Bonanza, The Adams Family, The Brady Bunch, The Partridge Family, Leave It To Beaver...*you betcha,' and they're worth bringing back from the sit-com cemetery to live again. Have you had the fortune, and I do mean fortune, of tuning in your tube to one of these vintage shows? The networks have begun to air these oldies but goodies on weekday afternoons. Some shows are in black and white, the clothes worn is so out-dated it's back in style, and the hair-do's are real doosers. The plots are simple, the pace is slow, the sets simple, the humor tired and the language clean. Do yourself a favor and feast your fancy on one of these re-runs soon, soon, very soon. They're so bad, they're good. I suppose the thinking behind the network big shots' decision is to appeal to those older generations who grew up watching these shows. To be honest, it's not a bad way of getting viewers to watch a little tube in their busy daily schedules. Even though the targeted audience may be a little older and grayer, they still have a memory that works.

I'm glad that God doesn't like to watch old re-runs of us and our mess-ups. You have a Creator that has all the capability (like a computer) and technology (like a laboratory) and storage space to retain the films of us falling short in our Christian walks. God could very easily air our sins back to us at judgment day. He could keep a little list of the times we chose our way and not His. He could point out just how big of a scab we all are and make us feel like an old shoe. He could keep the score in this game and I bet we'd see we lose by a lot. Guess what? He doesn't! He says that after we confess and repent of them, He takes all our bloopers and throws them so far that even man can't measure the distance. Correct me if I'm wrong here, but that's one heck of a throw, and I'm glad. Heaven doesn't show re-runs! And God seems to have a bad memory too!

GROW! How far is east from west? When does God throw our sins away? Do you have some you need chunked? What does this gift do for your relationship with Him?

READY, "His calamity will come suddenly and instantly he will be broken." Proverbs 6:15

SET, Growing up in a big city, they were as normal as flies at a picnic, but now living in a small country town, they are as noticeable as a ketchup stain on a white shirt. I'm talking about the scream of sirens. When you hear one while in a car, you're supposed to pull over and give right of way, but when you're on a street corner all you do is stop, look, and wonder. Sirens only show up in our lives when something bad is in the process of happening. It may mean a fire, wreck, heart attack, shooting, or funeral procession, but you can bet it's not for a birthday party. Usually the people who become directly involved with a siren are either scared, mesmerized, hysterical, crying, confused, or just plain terrified. Count on it, you *will* hear one or more in due time with the direction our country is headed. The final destination of the siren won't be a chill-out moment in time. Rest assured that the folks involved need more than a fire hose or paramedics...they need God.

Whether you hear them as loud as you do those on top of a police car or not, they are still there. These siren sounds come dressed in a little different shape and are presented in a random package. It may sound like an outburst of anger or a cutting remark. You may see them drunk or high at a party, or it may reveal itself by leaving a twenty-year marriage with a wife and two kids, but it's a siren. You see, sirens are nothing more than an attitude which emits an action as a warning signal. You hear and see them far more than you do the flashing lights. We have become so callused to them we have grown accustomed to their ways and accept them as a 'norm.' *False!* Wrong answer...we need to realize they are a cry for help, and we need to be of assistance as much as we would if we were performing CPR. Be alert at all times for people sirens in your life. Be attentive to what is going on in the arenas in which you live. Be a useful hand of God to a world falling apart. And...the next time you hear a siren, I hope your eyes and ears perk up like a dog's to a signal of help needed.

GROW! What are the siren sounds you hear the most? How do your friends cry out for help? Are you willing to help?

Up In Smoke

READY, *"Lift up your eyes to the sky, then look to the earth beneath, for they sky will vanish and all will go up in smoke, and the earth will wear out like a garment and its inhabitants will die in like manner, but my salvation shall be forever." Isaiah 51:6*

SET, We had pinched our pennies, collected our cash, and socked away savings for years to build our dream. The sacrifices had been many and the spending sprees few, but what we had done it for was worth the wait...*a home.* To map out the details, draw out the blueprints, decide on the tile, pick the paint, plot the location was all a part of the journey. To build *your* home is to be a part of the American dream. To cut out pictures from *Better Homes and Gardens* and tour other newly built homes, gathering ideas was a total blast. I never in my wildest dreams could believe we were actually going to meet with a home builder (contractor) to fulfill these dreams. It took a lot of wood, cement and nails, but four months later we went from soil to structure.

We had lived in our home about eighteen months when one September afternoon I received a phone call from my panicked wife that our home was on fire. That's right, up in smoke with no hope to put out the blaze before total destruction. We lost everything in a matter of moments...all we owned were the clothes on our backs and an alive family. A few months before the fire, a friend had told me, "Hold everything you have with open hands." God does give and take away, and all you have for the rest of your life is strictly on a rental basis. "Why did this happen to me?", I'd ask myself. To teach me that your job on this planet is to have joy when we get and keep that same joyful attitude when it's taken back, like Job. Take some simple advice form me, what you have, and will have, is okay, *but* it's a gift from God, and really all that matters is your relationship with Him.

GROW! How tightly do you hold what is yours? Do you see it as yours or God's? What helps you hold material items with a loose grip?

READY, *"He who has found his life shall lose it but he who has lost his life for my sake shall find it." Matthew 10:39*

SET, If you've ever been snow skiing, you're gonna' appreciate and relate to this story. A group of college folks went on a ski trip to Colorado during Christmas break and were greeted with record setting snowfall. The ski conditions had been ideal, tons of snow, blue skies and warm temperatures. The last day of skiing they all decided to catch the last lift of the day up to the top of the mountain and have a race down to the warming hut. They sat at the top until most skiers were out of sight so they would have the mountain to themselves and be clear for take-off. There were no rules on how, just be the first down and you win. Off they went in a downhill tuck position, any run they wanted, but fast. One of the guys was a real tree basher, so he decided to go the shorter way down through an avalanche roped-off area. Later on, all the group met at the hut, only to notice that one guy hadn't made it down, and it was nearly dark. They quickly warned ski patrol of the M.I.A.S. (missing-in-action skier) and set out to find him. The patrol returned late, unsuccessful, and decided to send out a trained rescue dog to find him. The young man had gotten lost and when night fell had decided to build a lean-to and sleep. The dog found the young man who had experienced hypothermia and was slipping into a deadly state of sleep with no awakening. The dog was trained to find the victim, lay on top of him to warm him, and stay there until help arrived. The dog's warm temperature brought the young man out of his frozen sleep to awake with some furry creature on him. He panicked and stabbed the dog to death with a nearby ski pole.

Did you realize that Jesus found you in a state of death and covered you with His blood He shed on the Cross in order to revive you back to a living state called eternity with God? Jesus' sole purpose was to save the unsaved, love the unlovable, and rescue the lost. He did it all for you, then he died. It's a hard thing to think, but yes, you had to kill Him so He could save you. What a hero!

GROW! Have you ever been lost with no hope? Did you realize that Jesus is the ultimate rescue team?

READY, *"And hope does not disappoint us, because God has poured out his love into our hearts by the Holy Spirit, whom he has given us."* Romans 5:5

SET, Now, here is a classic. Do you remember the childhood movie about the circus elephant with the enormous ears? How, at first he was mocked and abused by some (the crows), and then, he was praised and applauded by all (the crowd)? Dumbo is a classic, because it shows how an apparent goof can become a gift. The circus mouse plays a key role in the movie as the one who initiates the forward progress. He has a desire for Dumbo with expectations of success. He looks past the obvious to see the hope. Realize that hope will never disappoint you. How does the mouse pull this off? What else...the *magic feather.* Remember that it was Dumbo's belief in the feather which allowed him to soar through the air with the greatest of ease.

You and I have a responsibility to be like the mouse and desire others to be better than ourselves. Set goals to serve the servants, delegate yourself out of a job, to be a 'give fanatic' (anything to anyone). Give what you're asking...magic feathers, of course. That little something extra which will encourage someone else to succeed (maybe before you do). It's not the final destination that is so exciting, it's the journey. It's not the final bang but every step along the way. Give out feathers on the journey and not at the finish line. You realize that to do this you'll need the mind set of Christ (think like Him). Jesus succeeded, because He had hope in Heaven with His Father. When the world tells you to put all your hope in money, clothes, cars, medicine, houses, jobs, etc., you'll have to fight the thought and focus on the truth. Our hope in Christ is the promise of tomorrow. Dumbo may have started out his career as the brunt of jokes, but he ended up the talk of the town with a little help from a hope giver (the mouse) with a magic wand (the feather).

GROW! What is a magic feather to you? What magic feather can you give to someone else today?

What's Up With This?

READY, *"For it is better, if God will it so, that you suffer for doing what is right rather than for doing what is wrong." 1 Peter 3:17*

SET, You talk about a situation or circumstance that is best described as 'stinky.' Have you (and I'm sure you have) ever had the finger pointed at you for doing something you *didn't* do? It was probably one of those backward judicial systems that says you're guilty until proven innocent. Granted, in my own personal life, I would be considered your basic, strong-willed, free spirited, hell raiser by society (and my parents), so this situation didn't happen to me much. If you came into a crowed room of people looking for the guilty party it wouldn't have been a bad pick if you singled me out. There are those angels of our society (like you I'm sure) that seem to always be innocent because it's someone else's fault.

You know, ol' Peter had an interesting perspective on this finger pointing stuff and the scape goats of society that would be totally opposite of what one might expect. He states that if God puts (or allows) you in a situation where you are pronounced guilty of a crime (or act) that you never committed it's *good* (a blessing). Get that? Good...I mean read it with your own eye-balls and see for yourself. It is looked at as a blessing to suffer the consequences that someone else should be taking. I see that God views it as *better* for this sort of thing to happen to you than the other. Now, if I read this right, it's gonna' take a strong faith (and cool temper) to survive this crash with cruelty. So the next time you're strolling down life's merry highway and get broadsided, jump out and praise God for another opportunity to show you are different as a believer. What an incredible witness this will be and only a real Christian can pull it off.

GROW! When was the last time you were accused of doing wrong when in fact you hadn't? How did you react? Was it God's way or the natural way? Why would it be a blessing by God to be blamed when you're *not* guilty?

Throw Up!

READY, *"This book of the law shall not depart from your mouth, but you shall **meditate** on it day and night, so that you may be careful to do according to **all** that is written in it, for then you will make your way prosperous and then you will have success." Joshua 1:8*

SET, Being a father, I have heard some of the most creative one-liners imaginable. Each night when we go to bed with the kids, we talk a lot, memorize some, and pray a little. At times we read out of the children's Bible I love, because it's so simple and has bunches of pictures to boot. I recall a picture moment comment when we were talking about Moses throwing down the scepter which turned into a snake. Daniel (my oldest) looked at me with those big brown eyes and said, "Come on Dad, you're kidding." You can imagine at the age of four how hard it would be to fathom a stick (which he plays with often) turning into a snake.

We, as adults, occasionally have a hard time, even after we read it, accepting that God really expects us to believe Him. Come on God, that's not in there, is it? Sex before marriage, gluttony, lustful thoughts, gossip, causing someone to stumble, mediocrity, are all sin. God has to mean those things are just *bad*, not a *sin*. We are called to do all (and live by) that which is documented in scripture, and we are to meditate on it twenty four hours a day. Meditate means to 'throw up' throughout the day, in our lives and hearts. It's similar to a cow throwing up what she had eaten previously (her cud) and chewing on it again to retrieve more nutrition from it. When you read a verse or passage, do you recall it (throw it up) later to gain more wisdom to live like Christ? Why not? We should, because then we *will be* prosperous and successful in God's eyes whatever we have on our agenda during the day. Take a big chomp of scripture and try to meditate on it all day...you'll have a great day!

GROW! What did you read today out of the word? How can you practically remember it throughout the day? What will remind you to do this?

READY, *"A man's gift makes much room for him, and brings him before great men." Proverbs 18:16*

SET, You know, there has been a concept that has perplexed people for generations and it is that the same car that gets ya' there can also total you. Let me explain now what this wacko statement is talking about. You and everyone else who is made in the likeness of God has gifts that you've been given. Look at this list of natural gifts and see where you fit in (and you will)!

Leadership
Encouragement
Serving
Giving
Teaching
Motivating
Discernment
Administration
Organizing
Speaking
Mercy

No matter where you fit into this list, you are a walking bag of talented bones whether you admit it or not. Now, here is the part that is so tough to grasp and that is, over time you'll find that your (and others') strongest gift(s) *can become* (not will be) your biggest weakness too. Marriage counselors will warn you in pre-marriage meetings that what attracts you most to your future spouse could become a problem that begins to pull you apart. Satan, if we are not careful, gets a hold of our gifts and deceives us into using them for the wrong purpose or reason. Now this is nothing for you to lose sleep over tonight but it is a critical area that deserves some attention and a watchful eye. One of the keys to our happiness and joy here on earth is utilizing the gifts God has given us for the purpose of Kingdom building. Just be careful not to let the wrong one at the controls to take your biggest strength and steer it into your most frightful weakness.

GROW! What would you say are two of your biggest strengths? What are two of your biggest weaknesses? How can you prevent this process from happening in your life?

SHOWROOM TO JUNKYARD

READY, *"Glorify God with your body."* *1 Corinthians 6:20*

SET, I know the answer to this question before I even ask it, but let me give it a try. Have you ever taken a tour of an automobile junk yard? If yes, you're weird, if no, you've missed out. I'll betcha' that Henry Ford, after he first invented the motorized buggy, never dreamed his little idea would take off like it has. Basically the whole city of Detroit exists because of the mass production of automobiles, hence it's name, 'Motor City, USA.' We have junk yards nowadays about every twenty miles and in some cases they really trash up the landscape. Junk yards, as the slang term goes, are full of frames, lights, tailgates, transmissions, seats, tires and wheels, gear shifters, engine blocks, and much more. Vehicles wind up in a junk yard because they were either totaled in a wreck or just sold as scrap metal from a poorly taken care of auto. No matter what the reason, it's definitely not what a car has in mind when it thinks of 'shining on the showroom floor.'

Ripley's Believe It or Not, I am going to make a simile (show comparison) from this word picture and our world. I got to thinking how folks start off with *no* miles, dents, or oil usage, just like a new car. Let me explain...we all are born new and ready to run, but as time goes on we do things to our bodies (and engines) that tend to wear down their longevity and nullify the warranty. Whether it's stress relating to working too hard, drugs, alcohol, smoking, eating poorly, playing a sport that we shouldn't play, or whatever, it still adds up to the depreciation of our bodies. Of course, we don't call them junk yards, we call them hospitals and rest homes, but they both serve the same purpose. Don't do me the favor, do it for you and God. Think about what you're doing to your body before you do it. 'Just do it' can do more harm than good at times and you only have *one* body here on earth so treat it like a temple, not a piece of junk. There's nothing quite like a fine runnin' car but better yet even is a well-maintained earth suit.

GROW! Do you take good care of your body? In what areas could you improve? How can you improve *your temple of God?* Make a list of goals that will help you to keep focused and disciplined.

READY, *"Fixing our eyes on Jesus the author and perfector of our faith." Hebrews 12:2*

SET, Several years ago when the University of Colorado began its reign as a football dynasty, an interesting ritual involving the quarterback began. The starting quarterback this particular season had been a back-up for the previous few seasons to an all-conference quarterback. The relationship of the two was competitive, yet friendly. The graduating senior had done a great job of modeling just what a winning quarterback looked like and how one played. What the young quarterback didn't know was that his hero had cancer and would be watching the games from the press box this season. As the younger quarterback excelled along with the team during the season, he began a tradition. Every time he scored a touchdown he would abruptly look up at the press box and point his finger, as if to say, "That one was for you, bro.'" What an awesome sight to see a guy dedicate his entire season and what ended up being an illustrious career to his teammate/coach.

Whether we like football or not, we all go through life making victories. Some folks seem to be a human highlight film of successes. Everyone, whether they admit it or not, has a hero or mentor to whom they dedicate not their season, but their life. The question I have for you is, who do you point at? When you score, make a grade, get an honor, land a great job, find the mate of your dreams, get promoted, or whatever, who do you give the credit to? Who do you try to impress or live up to daily? We all have a reason to point at something. We all have a 'thing' we point at up on a pedestal. We all want to do something for someone. Who is it in your life? Put God up in the press box of your playing fields. Make Jesus your hero and your teammate/coach, because He is. Allow your glory moments to matter for God and not for someone who you may never live up to. Hey, and after you get in the habit of scoring big for God and giving Him the ol' point...turn around and spike it for the Savior. Yeah!

GROW! Who do you point at after you score in life? Who gets all your glory moments? How can Jesus be seen in the press box of your life? Will you allow Him to receive it?

It Will Find You Out

READY, "And the Lord called to the man and said to him, 'Where are you?' And he (Adam) said, 'I heard the sound of You in the garden and I was afraid because I was naked, so I hid.' And He replied 'Who told you that you were naked?'" Genesis 3:9-11

SET, It didn't take me long to break one of the Ten Commandments at the young age of ten, but I did it. I had just received one of those (what I thought at the time) manly items for my birthday...a cap gun. Listen up now, because this assault weapon could make your ears ring like you'd just walked out of some rock concert. I mean, this was one of those heavy duty plastic jobs with the fake red barrel for visual effect. Only one small problem to overcome upon its arrival to me as a gift...no caps. That's right, my mom didn't quite get all the necessary items for me to reap havoc on my neighbors and sister (ha ha). The cost of one roll of caps was a dollar twenty-five, but I had no money in my piggy bank. The next day I accompanied my mom to Safeway (a grocery store) to pick up some milk and eggs. There I decided to permanently borrow from the toy rack a roll of caps. That's right, the old five finger discount, or you might just say stealing. I was successful in my first heist...until my mom asked me that fatal question. No, she didn't see me do it, or hear me shoot my gun (I may be dumb, but I'm not stupid). She simply asked me if I wanted to earn some allowance so I could buy some caps for my gun. My conscience was eating a hole in my stomach like battery acid on a tee shirt. I immediately broke down crying and confessed my offense in detail.

In the Garden of Eden, Adam and Eve knew they had done wrong and were guilty. It's the first time in the history of mankind we see that *sin produces self-consciousness.* God knew what they had done, but you read in Genesis 2:25 that they were naked and *not* ashamed until now. This is why God immediately knew they had done wrong by the simple fact they were hiding and ashamed to be naked. Sin causes us to look at ourselves and not others. It forces us (by guilt) to give ourselves away because we *want* to be found out to relieve the strain of guilt on our hearts. Take my word for it...your sin will find you out.

GROW! How do you react when you're not right with God? What makes you self-conscience?

A Second Chance

READY, "*Now the word of the Lord came to Jonah the second time saying 'Arise and go.'*" *Jonah 3:1-2*

SET, Aren't you glad we are not dictated by a God who is one of those '1-2-3 strikes you're out' of the old ball game? Can you imagine if His love was totally conditional and we were only graded pass, fail? I love the stories in scripture that confirm the curriculum in God's classroom, and that is a test with second chances. Over and over you'll find situations like David, Noah, Adam, Moses, and many others that were given another chance at learning a lesson the hard way and getting another shot at passing the course. Our classrooms are filled with teachers who are so 'matter of fact' it's scary. I love the quote, "If at first you don't succeed, try, try again." God continually, through a super natural x-ray vision, sees right to the core of our hearts and desires and judges us there. A wise man once said, "You can tell the worth of a person by the number of failures he has overcome." How true that is also in God's perspective of teaching His students.

I'm sure you all are familiar with the story of Jonah and the whale, so I won't bore you with the details, but I will refresh your cranium. If you look at Jonah 1:2 and 3:1 you'll notice it's as if God has a stutter problem. He says the same thing twice, just a chapter apart. Why? What went on in there? I'll tell you in *Reader's Digest* condensed version format. Jonah jumped on the wrong ship to Tarshish, hid below deck, a whopper of a storm blew in, the sailors were confused and threw over their luggage, Jonah took a cat nap, the captain found the slacker sleeping, chunked Jonah overboard with no lifevest, Charlie the Tuna (whale) swallowed him, got indigestion and threw him up on a beach and Jonah learned two things: obey God and fish burp smells.

Despite running like a chicken, hiding like a snake and swimming like a rock, God gave Jonah another chance. The same God in this story gives you a second chance daily to obey His instructions. Learn quickly and who knows, maybe you won't get gobbled up by a carp and have to start over where you began. Life is much easier this way, you know, just as Jonah.

GROW! Do you thank God for second chances? Do you learn from your mistakes?

THE MILKY WAY

READY, "*I gave you milk to drink, not solid food, for you were not yet able to receive it.*" *1 Corinthians 3:2*

SET, It won't be until that day that you have your first child that you will truly understand. You'll find out, in the world of resources, that there is still yet a lot you'll learn through experience about having a baby. Never did or could I imagine what a joyful 'job' it was to maintain a kid. I mean these bubbly bouncing balls of baby blubber are an adventure to experience. Basically, all they do in their first six months of existence is eat, sleep, poo-poo and cry all the time. Every now and then you can uncross their baby blue eyes and get a goo-goo-ga-ga accompanied with a cock-eyed grin, but life stays pretty routine for the most part. The only food they consume in their early months is milk. You know, the stuff like the Wonder Bread commercial says "builds strong bodies twelve ways." No vegetables (yuk), no chocolate sundaes, no T-bone steaks, no double cheese burgers with fries, not even a pep-peroni pizza (what a drag)...just milk!

In this excerpt of scripture the apostle Paul is speaking after his visit and through his first letter to the church in Corinth. What he is saying, in layman's terms, is that there are folks who are baby believers who are not yet ready for tougher scripture steaks. There is nothing wrong with that—just as it would be foolish to try to force feed meat to a little newborn right out of the incubator. Some people who are new to the faith and family of God should be allowed the right of 'growing up in Christ' just as they grew up into an adult. Don't choke new Christians on information or doc-trine that they just can't digest yet. Don't force them to deal at the same level as someone who has been a believer for five years. Give them, (they deserve it), the right to mature at God's pace, not your pace. Believe you me, feeding too much is as bad as not feeding enough, and who knows...you'll probably end up getting it burped back at you. Remember, also, that babies grow at different rates.

GROW! What sort of spiritual supplements should you feed a new Christian? How important is it that you allow them to grow up at God's pace? Do you feed the wrong food to baby believers? What happened?

READY, *"Now to Him who is able to do exceedingly abundantly beyond all that we ask or think, according to His power that works within us." Ephesians 3:20*

SET, Like it or not, the amount of money changing hands from betters to bookies every day is astronomical. Individuals bet on golf matches, sports events, horse and dog races, lottery tickets, poker games, slot machines, and the roll of dice. If you've ever been to Las Vegas, you've witnessed first hand enough money being lost to pull this country out of its national debt. I once heard a professional gambler say, "I never meet anyone ever satisfied...they've either not won enough or lost all they had." The world in which you exist is continually trying to persuade you to bet your life on sex, looks, possessions, money, or chemical highs. Some do win the 'jackpot' but most come up empty handed and defeated in more areas than the pocket book. This roulette wheel we spin each day called life is more than winning or losing money, it's your life.

Let's bring this illustration home by asking a very important question. What are *you* betting *your* life on? What machine, table, arena, or race do you set high stakes on? We are all looking to find the pot of gold that sits at the end of every rainbow, right? We all search high and low for that one jackpot that will supposedly bring us joy and happiness, but what's our guarantee that we'll win? Jesus takes the guessing out of the game by making our stakes attainable by a simple commitment, not a wad of money or a handful of chips. He eliminates the anxiety by taking upon Himself the stress of the wager (life). Jesus comes to give us an abundance of life, which means by dictionary terms 'more than enough.' Isn't it a dream come true, pot of gold, and jackpot to know that He is our provider for a life in paradise after this life? Go ahead, place your bet, roll the dice, spin the wheel, but make sure it's on Christ for the sure win.

GROW! What are you betting your life on? What makes your face smile most in life? Can God provide you with the ultimate jackpot in the long run? How?

READY, *"For this reason a man shall leave his mother and father and cleave to his wife and the two shall become one in marriage."* Genesis 2:24

SET, The liberal arm of our present population says that American teens can't stop having sex, so condom distribution is the solution to the AIDS problem. The real problem comes in the 'buying in to' of a sense of false security way of thinking that a condom is a legitimate answer. Not to mention the fact that there hasn't been protection provided for the guilt ridden mind and reputation of the user. The simple answer is that sex education (in this form) usually means nothing more than sex instruction and a ticket to let experience be the teacher, verses the parent(s). Take a minute and look over the following facts...look *hard.*

Experts have identified 55 different sexual diseases.
Teens account for 25% all sexually transmitted diseases.
56 million people are infected today with a sexually transmitted disease
Each year about 150,000 women become infertile as a result of sexually transmitted diseases.
The national average of American 15 year-olds having sex is 41%.
Condoms fail to prevent pregnancy 15% of the time.
43% of unwanted pregnancies happen to people using birth control devices. Half of those end up in abortion.
Since 1970 the U.S. government has spent 3 billion dollars to promote 'safe sex.'
Between 1970 and 1991 the number of unwed teen moms rose 68%.
3 out of 10 HIV positive persons using condoms transmit HIV to their partners.
Reasons teens gave for not having sex: 65% disease, 62% fear of pregnancy, 50% worry of parents...teen sex, not for love.
Condoms break down due to temperature or lubricants and gels.
By the time a child finishes high school he's spent 18,000 hours with TV and 12,000 hours in school (average only 25 minutes a week with parents).

Let the facts alone, not to mention the biblical truths, speak loudly. To wait until the context of a committed marriage is to say "I loved you before I ever met you." Commit today to wait and abstain from sex before marriage until God brings you your knight in shining armor or princess in a tower.

GROW! Just how safe are condoms? What does 'safe sex' really mean? Why abstain? Why wait until marriage? What does the Bible say about premarital sex? Who invented sex? Why?

DOUBLE THINKIN'

READY, *"Abraham believed God and it was reckoned to him as righteousness." Romans 4:3*

SET, Einstein was quoted as saying that humans only use ten percent of the capability of their brains. Now, it's a good thing he didn't know me, or that percentage would have probably been less. I'd say he's pretty close on his assumption. If old Albert could see us now, he would be pretty impressed with us sending men to the moon, car designs, aeronautics, medical breakthroughs, and technology. We have folks we walk by daily that are smarter than whips, and we don't even know about it. Who knows, you may be living with the next Nobel Prize winner and not even have a clue. Although, at times, we have a tendency in our nature to overdo our gifts and they end up getting us in a lot of trouble. Our brains are invented and given to us individually with the specific purpose to glorify Him, but not try to figure Him or His ways out.

A process that some go through in their thinking and exercising that muscle in their skulls is called 'double thinking.' Now, this would be best identified as thinking things over and over until they become obsessed with the thought. In other words, trying to figure out every why we come across in life. Don't get me wrong now, we are supposed to be slow to act and quick to listen and analyze, but we shouldn't overdo it. Take for instance, the uselessness in trying to figure out why only the good folks die young, or losing all you own to a fire, or national disasters, or wars, or heaven and hell. Let me give you a bit of advice...faith *cannot* be figured out, or it wouldn't be real faith. Hebrew 11:1 states that faith is "the assurance of things hoped for, the conviction of things not seen." God cannot possibly reveal all His knowledge or His plans to you, because your brain would explode. We, as midget mortals, don't have the cranium capacity to handle such wisdom. So the next time you begin to double think, take note and relax knowing that you are in good hands with God...not All-State!

GROW! Have you ever tried to figure out God's why's? What things do you 'double think' about the most? Does it help or hurt your faith?

READY, *"It would be better for him to tie a millstone around their neck and be thrown into the sea than to cause the least of the little ones to stumble." Luke 17:2*

SET, Let the facts speak for themselves:

Eight million teens use alcohol regularly.
Alcohol related incidents kill ten thousand ages sixteen to twenty-four each year.
The number one killer of teens today is alcohol.
Forty-one percent of all college students consume five alcoholic drinks in a row each week.
Sixty-four percent of all violent crimes on college campuses are alcohol related.
Alcohol abuse kills brain cells.
Thirty-five percent of all academic problems relate to alcohol.
(USA Today News)

You sure don't have to be a rocket scientist to see that alcohol in America has become a huge problem. In 1990, a survey of college presidents by the Carnegie Foundation found that alcohol was "the most serious problem we face on our campus today." There are six hundred and thirty-seven references to drink and drinking in the Bible. In those, there are thirteen different words (translations) for wine. We all can read that it's wrong to drink 'strong drink' or to be 'drunk,' but what about casual drinking? We need to see that in the Bible the translations for wine are yayin, shekar, and tirosh; and in the New Testament they are sikera and gleukos. All words for wine are equivalent to our modern day meaning for grape juice. The water to wine made biblical wine about two percent alcohol (our wine today has eleven to twenty percent alcohol) and during biblical times was considered nothing more than purified water. By comparison, modern brandy is twenty percent alcohol and other hard liquor is forty to fifty percent alcohol.

You can state all the facts you want, but the best reason to abstain is...*it just don't look right*. To compromise a lifestyle for a quick fix or social image is a gamble you can't afford to lose. Step back, count the cost, weigh the pluses and minuses, and take a radical stand for the cause of Christ. If you're gonna' be a light, don't be a Bud Light!

GROW! Why should you not drink alcohol? What does it do for your image? Why do you feel most people drink?

READY, *"We will sing for joy over your victory, and the name of our God will set up our banners. May the Lord fulfill all your petitions."* Psalm 20:5

SET, Nothing is sweeter than victory. In 1979 I had the privilege of playing on the University of Oklahoma Big 8 Championship team, when we advanced to the final sixteen teams in the NCAA tournament. It was a difficult year filled with thrills and spills, but the outcome was worth the long hours and achy muscles. It took the unity of fifteen players, an inner strength of determination, and a never quit attitude to get where we were. That year I learned that victory is not an emotional high but a steady vision, not an automatic inheritance, not an unattainable dream, not an independent achievement, not something that just happens to you while you passively wait. I realized that victory included taking *aim* on goals and working daily to achieve those goals, one step at a time. I understood that with no *discipline* there would be no victories to enjoy. I learned that *action* was needed to conquer the mountains we were destined to face. And lastly, that the rewards were worth the wait.

I don't think that Jesus, while hanging on the cross, intended us, as followers, to come in second place. I think He wanted us to experience the thrill of victory and realize that the agony of defeat is part of the process. The three things you must have in the victory as a Christian are birth, faith, and truth. We have been given the opportunity to experience all these and use them in our arenas. In this world, there is never a guaranteed success, but in our faith walk there is. Wow! What a deal...you are guaranteed a victory if you play by the rules (Bible) and have a head coach named Jesus Christ. Now that makes those trophies and medals look like mere trinkets.

GROW! When was the last time you experienced a victory in Christ? Did you act as excited then as you do when a team wins a championship?

YOUR NEIGHBOR

READY, *"Love your neighbor as yourself." Matthew 22:39*

SET, I've always wondered just exactly who my neighbor is. Does this command really mean the family that lives to my right or left? Do you find it as hard as I do to love some folks at all? They delight and distract, they demand patience, they are people of confidence and conflict, they love us then leave us, they understand then judge us. We start talking to God and pointing out to Him things like, "But God, have you ever met my neighbor?" or "Hey God, I'll tithe my ten percent, but witness too?" Remember the old song, "They will know we are Christians by our love, by our love; yes, they'll know we are Christians by our love"? To obey this command we must first look at two things. First, what does love mean, and second, who is our neighbor? I heard a quote that states "love is like a ghost few have seen but a lot talk about." Another one is "love is like a creeping vine, it withers if it has nothing to cling to."

The love God is taking about and models best is *agape*. In other words, a love with no strings attached, not based on conditions of performance. Secondly, our 'neighbor' could be defined as the people God puts in our life every day of our life. Folks like gas station attendants, garbage men, short tempered drivers, teachers who fail you, police who give out speeding tickets, a locker mate, politicians, folks we just plain don't like. You must possess sensitivity and sacrifice of self to attain this command. We all know we love ourselves (a lot) and that if we actually loved others as much as we adore our own selves it would be quite the sight. Try it today and see if you don't end up feeling better about yourself and your example to an afflicted world who hates more than it loves. What an awesome impact it will be if we actually take this command and live it out in our daily lives. Go on...try it, you'll like it. Who knows...you may need to start with the person next door.

GROW! Who are your neighbors in your life? How can you actually love unconditionally? Did Jesus model this lifestyle? How? Can you? When? Today? Go for it!

116

I Give You My Word

READY, *"Let your yes be yes and your no be no." James 5:12*

SET, The Boy Scout Oath: "On my honor I will do my best to do my duty to God and my country and to obey the Scout Law; to help other people at all times; to keep myself physically strong, mentally awake, and morally straight."

There it is, just as easy to quote now as it was when I was younger. This oath is what every Boy and Girl Scout promises to live. This life in which we live is full of oaths. You see it when the President of the United States takes office, you repeat it before you take the witness stand in a court of law, you'll be in awe of it when two people are exchanging rings at the altar for marriage, and you read it when Moses came down from Mt. Sinai glowing after his encounter with God Almighty. I realize that saying and living are on two sides of the freeway. It's one thing to put your hand up or mumble the words, but following through and committing to what you just said is tough.

We seem to have lost something other than our wallet or car keys from prior generations. I'm not sure if they forgot to teach us, we didn't listen, or maybe we just don't see the value in it. What? Your *word.* It's a rare quality to see surviving today when someone gives you his word and also follows through with the commitment. When someone says he will be there at 2:00 o'clock and he arrives ten minutes early, and you can bet on it. In a society of red tape and paper work, we could sure do ourselves a favor by closing out business contracts with a handshake and a verbal commitment instead of a novel of words. How about teachers giving you a test and letting you take it home on your word that you won't cheat, or committing to your date's parents that you will go where you promise to go? Promises and oaths are interchangeable words, and whether you're a Scout or a Christian they are worth taking and keeping for the rest of your life.

GROW! How good is your word? Why is it so tough to commit to a promise? Is your word good today?

WARNING LABELS

READY, *"By faith Noah, when being warned about things not yet seen, in holy fear built an ark to save his family. By his faith he condemned the world and became heir of the righteousness that comes by faith." Hebrews 11:7*

SET, You see them everywhere if you look closely. They inform, encourage and instruct concerning possible dangers. What are they? *Warning Labels.* You've seen them on medicines, chemicals, sports equipment, electric devices and on heavy machinery. Their purpose is like the ol' saying goes, "an ounce of prevention is worth a pound of cure." If you defy them, you could be harmed or possibly, even killed. If you play with fire you will probably get burned...if you don't heed the warning you'll probably feel the effects. Why is it that our old self steps in and whispers lies to us like, "Go ahead, it couldn't be that bad," or, "Step out, take a chance, live life to its fullest.'

God's word is full of thousands of warning labels to communicate the dangers ahead and describe the hazards that could occur if overlooked. Isn't it great that we have a Master who looks out for us more than we do? What an awesome way of showing one's love for another! How incredible it is to tell others of potential potholes on life's highways and byways. The real question is do you listen and obey them? Do you actually take the warnings from your navigator (God) that bad weather could be ahead if you continue flying as you are? Begin today to read the labels (in the Bible), heed the warnings, and obey your spiritual instinct. Who knows...someday they will probably save your life.

GROW! What warning label did you read today in the scripture? How does it apply now? With whom can you communicate what you've learned?

READY, *"In those days Israel had no king, and everyone did what was right in their own eyes." Judges 21:25*

SET, The sport of track is one of history prior. It is amazing how endurance, speed, and quickness play such a pivotal role in this competition between individuals. It is one of these sports that at the end of the race, you can't blame coming in last on another teammate for missing the shot, fumbling the ball, duffing a serve, or whiffing a pitch. As this sport evolved, new events were added to enhance the viewing and generate some flare for the public and the participants. The event...high jumping. I ask you, who would be creative enough (if that's what you'd call it) to come up with a sport where a person bounces over a bar, Fosberry Flops, and then pile drives themselves into a pit? Have you ever noticed that the way the winner is determined is by the continual movement of the bar up in height and the weeding out process of the jumpers not being able to jump over the advancing bar? What would happen if the bar wasn't needed and everyone was scored by their own standard? Talk about chaos, talk about disagreements. The bar is the standard which the participants have to shoot (jump) for in order to test themselves. As the bar moves up, the standard to conquer becomes more difficult to achieve, yet more rewarding to attain.

Can you imagine a world without a standard and a society without a Savior? You should, you're living in one as we speak. Our society seems to have drifted onto the rocks of destruction without notice. The Bible is full of past civilizations who seem to have come up with their own rules and ended up failing the test. Jesus is our standard, our world record holder, our model of excellence we are shooting for. Without Him going before us setting the scale, walking beside us, helping us compete, and following us up, and holding us accountable, we wouldn't make it. Don't get mad at the standard. It's there for you to shoot for, never lose hope in the King, He's the record holder. So what are you waiting on? It's your jump next!

GROW! How much do you prepare daily for attaining His standard? How much did you prepare today? (If not, then get after it!)

ONE MINUTE PLEASE!

READY, "I am an ambassador in chains, that in proclaiming it I may speak boldly, as I ought to speak." Ephesians 6:20

SET, This Sunday was like any other Sunday afternoon for the Smith family. Everyone came through the door after church shedding their church clothes like a St. Bernard sheds hair. Dad immediately went to the EZ-Boy recliner to snatch up the newspaper and remote control and kick back to watch NFL football while Mom was putting on her apron to fix a good old fashioned home cooked lunch for the family. Big Brother went outside to try out the new jump he had made for his skateboard and Little Sis was left with no attention at all. Mom said she didn't need any help in the kitchen, so Sis went to chat with ol' Dad during the commercials and between articles. The little girl tugs on Dad's shirt sleeve to be granted some attention and asks, "Daddy, do you think you could live like Jesus for one year?" The father folds up the paper and answers in his mega-voice, "No, honey, that is impossible to do." The little girl waits patiently until a time-out in the game, then interrupts her dad, asking, "Well then Dad, do you think you could live like Jesus for one month?" The father, a bit frustrated with the interruptions, answers in a harsh voice, "No! Now honey, you know Jesus was perfect and that we aren't. Run along and help Mom fix lunch." Upset but not defeated, the little girl walks a few feet, then abruptly turns and asks, "Okay then, do you think you could live just one minute like Jesus?" With smoke bellowing from his ears, Dad answers, "Okay, okay, okay! I guess we could live a whole minute just like Christ." To which the child replied, "Daddy, then why don't we live like Jesus one minute at a time?"

GROW! Why don't we try to live like Christ just one minute at a time? Why does our nature tell us to broad-jump instead of walk? How can we seriously live like Jesus each minute, each day? How can you live today like Him? Will you give it a go?

Half Full Or Half Empty

READY, *"Caleb quieted the people before Moses and said 'We should by all means go up and take possession of it, we shall overcome it.' But the other men had gone up with him too and said 'We are not able to go up against the people for they are too strong for us.'"* Numbers 13:30-31

SET, A great test to see if people are optimists or a pessimists is to show them a clear glass containing water up to the half-way point. Now ask if the glass is half empty or half full. You will find most of the time that the majority will view the glass of water as half empty. This is not wrong, just a fact. Most people always see situations in life as half empty too. The masses will, most of the time, see life's negatives far before they see its positives.

If you have ever read the story of Joshua and Caleb, you have read a story of two perspectives. In a nutshell God has told the people of Israel that the 'Land of Milk and Honey' is theirs for the taking. A bunch of spies (or scouts) are sent into the land of Canaan to check it out and bring back a report of its condition. They were to find out if the land was safe, had good pastures, grew good vegetation, and would be a good home for three million new Israelite residents. Of all the scouts only two came back positive; the rest saw a glass half empty. Yes, the land was perfect but it did have a few bugs to work out, namely, mean thugs called Amelikites who could be dealt with. God calls you daily to go into your home, school, clubs, team, or circle of friends and take a stand, take up residency for Him. Yes, it will be tough and there will be opposition, but remember He took care of them on the cross at Calvary. Will you return to Him as the majority with a half empty report or a Joshua and Caleb report of half full? Think about it.

GROW! How do you view the cup? Do you see more negative in God's plans or positive? Do you feel you are an overcomer and capable of accomplishing anything with Him? Why or why not?

READY, *"Better is an open rebuke than love that is concealed."* Proverbs 27:5

SET, Let me start this off by presenting you with a situation and see how you would respond. Let's say you were a real outdoor personality (tree bark eater) and you had lots of years experience hiking and camping in the southwest range of the Colorado Rockies (not the baseball team either). On this day you have invited a close friend to go and enjoy the clean air, vast beauty and sore muscles of a weekend backpacking experience. While walking on a two foot wide path on the northern face of a mountain some eleven thousand feet up, you encounter a shale slide area. Now, the pathway sets about three feet from (this sounds like a riddle) the edge of a thousand foot cliff on which many have slipped and plunged to death in prior expeditions. You saw your friend walking haphazardly (not paying much attention), about to come upon this risky, dangerous portion of the pathway. would you warn your friend of the upcoming danger, or just hope they made it on their own? I know this is a stupid question, but think about your answer.

Now, to tie this goofy illustration into a thought provoking point. You rub shoulders every day with friends, some acquaintances, and others who are about to take a dangerous plunge in their lives. This plunge could be in a relationship, bad judgment, or whatever. You, yes you, have the chance to warn (rebuke) this friend with and out of love before he slips off his mortal mountain to a decision of death. Self destruction is as prevalent in our world as flies in a cow barn. Don't be afraid to step out of your comfort zone and confront someone who needs some tender love on their decision making process. *Care* enough to risk the relationship for the rewards of agape love. Don't conceal your love; let it be active and useful in your relationships. Who knows, they may thank you later for saving their lives.

GROW! How much do you care for your friend(s)? Do you warn them of upcoming dangers? Why or why not?

CATCH THE VISION

READY, "Where there is no vision the people perish." Proverbs 29:18

SET, Years ago before Disney grew into the number one tourist attraction in North America, Walt Disney created a vision. During the building and before the completion of Disneyland in California, he put together a huge banquet/cookout which cost three million dollars for all the workers who would be involved in building this theme park. The plumbers, concrete layers, electricians, roofers, welders, painters, bull-dozer operators, surveyors, crane operators, and so on, were all gonna' be invited to this bash. Walt Disney had the architects design a small 'model' of the finished product, so that all these workers would be able to see it during the banquet. The purpose was to create a vision in the eyes of each worker so they just didn't hammer a nail, wire a building, weld some pipe, lay some concrete, survey the dirt, paint a building, or bull-doze a rock. After seeing the model, the workers wouldn't just put forth their muscle and effort, but also put their hearts into their work.

We, too, need to have a vision for *all* that we do in this life. We need to catch a dream of not just what we're doing but who we're doing it for and its purpose. You've got to have a vision for being a follower of Jesus, or your gas tank will run dry quickly. You've got to see the reason for waiting until marriage to have sex. You must see that there is a purpose for spending time in God's Word and praying to Him. See the light at the end of the tunnel today, and your path will be a lot easier to follow because of focusing on it. Believe you me, I think Disneyland is the neatest spot on earth, but it can't hold a candle to your spot in Heaven. It won't cost you a three million dollar banquet to catch this vision, just a little time spent in the Word. And who knows, maybe Mickey and Minnie will be waiting at those pearly gates greeting you on the way in.

GROW! Do you have a vision? Of what? How can a spiritual vision help you in your walk with Christ? How can it help you remain pure? Where can you catch this vision?

READY, *"For I was envious of the arrogant, as I saw the prosperity of the wicked." Psalm 73:3*

SET, Take a moment, open your Bible to Psalm 73:1-19 and read those few verses (read slowly and I'll be here when you're done). Wow! What a nugget of wisdom spoken by Asaph (no, that's not a brand of running shoe). Do you see what is going on here? Asaph is stricken with the thought that he perceives how the wrong people seem to be the ones who always get promoted. Isn't that true today? Think about it...when was the last time someone came up to you and asked for your autograph for following Christ daily? Now, I'm not saying that Christians are the scapegoat of society by any means, but I am saying that we live in a world that promotes worldly ways, not God's guidelines. It's the bad guys in the movies who are the ones riding off into the sunset on their horses. Asaph is so honest with God (I love it) and bares his soul and emotions in a Psalm. At times, you and I can become disheartened by the thought or questions of 'is it worth it'?

It is so ordinary for the dishonest, arrogant, unfaithful, unholy to seem like their paths are always paved with success. Don't be fooled into thinking that an ungodly lifestyle will not eventually destroy you (read verse 19). The benefits of being a Christian are numerous. Let's take a quick peep at just what those perks are:

He'll always be there. (verse 23)

He'll give you a testimony to see. (verse 28)

He'll meet all your needs. (verse 25)

He'll always guide you. (verse 24)

He'll give you a future in Heaven. (verse 24)

He'll hold your hand along the way. (verse 23)

Now, I'm not bright, but I can see that this is a life worth leading.

GROW! What frustrates you most about this world? How does God's way look to you? How can you encourage yourself when you get to wondering if it's worth it?

A Tongue Lashing

READY, "*They set their mouth against the heavens and their tongue parades loose through the earth.*" *Psalm 73:9* "*The Lord hates a lying tongue.*" *Proverbs 6:17*

SET, Take a look at the human anatomy for a moment. Look specifically at the head (neck up). Do you notice anything about the functions of the facial feature? Have you noticed that we all have two ears, a mouth, and one nose (I hope)? Do you see that you can close and open the mouth but not the ears? Why? Do you think it's just an assembly line mistake and God is soon to have a factory recall on everyone's face any day now? Growing up, I'm sure you hummed the tune of 'sticks and stones may break my bones, but words can never hurt me.' I bet the guy who wrote that must have been a hermit in a cave on a deserted island to have made up such a lie. Untruthful words can probably do more damage to a person than diving into an empty pool. The tongue has done more damage to the human race than the black plague or polio. With it we praise our friends then turn around and stab them in their back. Why, oh why?

The Bible says it's the bit in a horse's mouth, the spark that sets off a forest fire, and the poison of a cobra. To realize its power one must first realize it's whereabouts and where it hides...in your *mouth*. Self-image, reputation and potential can be all but destroyed by a few words of gossip. What defines the word gossip? Speaking to anyone about another person's business that are neither part of the solution or problem. It's trying to knock someone down a notch for selfish reasons. This is why God tells us to be quick to listen and slow to speak. Today's galloping gossips seem to have this verse flipped around. Learn to tame your tongue and put out rumors when they come to you, don't fuel their fire. Listen to yourself in a conversation with others and see if you're spreading a rumor, or stating a fact or fiction. Do yourself and others a favor by being a different breed of person and not letting that muscle in your mouth exercise on someone else's life.

GROW! Do you gossip? Do you say things to others in order to demean someone else? How can you begin to tame your tongue? How can you train it to speak the truth?

125

GETTING TO KNOW YOU

READY, *"But the very hairs of your head are all numbered."*
Matthew 10:30

SET, Talk about being really bored, listen to this. Years ago, a German scientist did a study and counted random people's hair content. The study showed that the number of hairs on a human head is linked to the color of the hair. There are more hairs on a black-haired person's head than a red-haired person's; more on a brown-haired person than black-haired; and more on a blonde-haired person than brown-haired. A black-haired female has about one hundred and ten thousand hairs, and a blonde about one hundred and forty thousand hairs on her head. The average female will lose up to one hundred hairs a day. A man daily shaves off about one sixty-fourth of an inch, and over a period of forty years will cut off twenty-five feet of beard. Wow, interesting stuff, huh?

Now, if you think that is a brain teaser, try this one. God knows exactly how many hairs *every* person living on this earth has on his head. What that translates to is not that He has a hang-up about hair, but He does make a career of caring. How awesome to think that God, the Creator of all this, is so flipped out about *you* that he even wants to know the details about *you.* I'll bet you a Yankee dime you don't know of one person (family, friend, or spouse) who knows that number. And guess what? No one is even gonna' waste his time to find it out either. I really feel that the reason this verse is even in the Bible is not to show you how smart God is, but to prove to you (which He doesn't have to do) that even the smallest, seemingly meaningless details about you, He cares about. Now, that is what I would call true love in its purest form.

GROW! How many hairs do you have on your head? Do you care? Then why do you think God does?

READY, *"Therefore confess your sins to one another, pray for one another, that you may be healed. The effective prayer of righteous man accomplishes much." James 5:16*

SET, Ask yourself this question real quick...what would it be like if I was alive when Jesus was? Can you even imagine? You wouldn't have to worry about hairstyles (they had no salons), the car you drove (no gas stations), what you wore (fluorescent was out), or career opportunities (not a lot offered). In that day life was so much simpler (I think) and less stressed-out than today. Folks two thousand years ago seemed to take life one step at a time, day by day, minute by minute. The current didn't seem to flow as fast, yet it still did flow. Folks still incurred problems and difficulties, whether it be sickness, survival, or what would be for supper. The way people of that culture dealt with tricks, impurity, and a hurting conscience was by confession, not necessarily to a priest or mediator, but to each other.

Do realize that if our society today would listen and act upon this scripture we would virtually put every psychologist and psychiatrist out of business? If we could learn to confess to God and others in our troubled times when we have fallen short, we would have no need for a shrink. Depression would be only a word we used to describe America in the Thirties. After you heard a confession then you would take some serious action and begin to pray for them and their needs so the healing process could begin. I realize this formula seems to be too simple to do any good but take it from 'The Man' and His counseling skills; it works wonders!

GROW! When was the last time you confessed a sin to a reliable friend? How did it feel? Why do you think counseling clinics are packed with clients today? What would this formula for freedom do for you in your relationship with Christ? Will you do it? Why not?

READY, *"Love your Lord God with all your heart, soul, and might."*
Deuteronomy 6:5

SET, You don't have to look too far to see the ol' pointer finger raised high parading the symbol for being number one. Each week, college and high school polls rank teams according to their previous records and recent performances. Tennis players, cheer leading squads, debate teams, all jockey for that prestigious spot of the top gun. To be number one in anything, whether it's sports, academia, or mutual funds is to let the facts speak loudly for themselves. The strange thing about being a lonesome dove at the top of the perch is that it's easier to get there than it is to stay up there. To hold that spot for very long takes a lot of dedication and determination on the team or individual's part.

Ted Koppel, while speaking at commencement at Duke University a few years ago, referencing the Ten Commandments, was quoted, "Moses didn't come down from Mt. Sinai with the Ten Suggestions." After Moses had a one-on-one meeting with the Father of Light and returned aglow, he had with him the 'Top Ten' in working order. In other words, the first command handed down from divine to domestic was to love God with all that you are. Let's take a second to look at the three areas God asked us to give Him as a deposit down on eternity. Number one is your heart, your pumper, your livelihood, your existence. Number two would be your soul which is made up of three areas, mind, will, and emotions. Number three concludes with might which is your energy, strength, and every muscle fiber you own in your earth suit. Listen, the number one ranking commandment is there for a reason, a good one too, because God knows if you love Him with all you can be, that you'll go places for Him. Love God first and all the other nine commandments will come easy. Remember too that these are commands, and not mere suggestions. God loves to stay atop the polls.

GROW! What do you love God with? How do you practically love God with all you have? How hard is it for you to love God first in your life and rank Him number one on your poll?

READY, "*The goal of our instruction is first love, from a pure heart, good conscience and sincere faith.*" *I Timothy 1:5*

SET, There is a famous NBA basketball star who played for the Boston Celtics throughout the Eighties. His name is Larry Bird. He was a star forward for Indiana State and fueled his college team to the 1979 NCAA National Championship showdown with none other that Michigan State, whose star was Magic Johnson. Larry then went on to a star studded, all-star career with the Celtics and led them to several World Championships in the late Eighties. The story is told of a pre-game warm-up session in which Larry was alone, shooting baskets at the Boston Garden a few hours prior to a playoff game with the LA Lakers. After shooting several shots and missing all of them, Larry called upon the arena manager to check to see if the basket was at the standard height of ten feet. The arena manager, proud of his dependability for doing things right the first time, was disgusted with Larry's questioning his capabilities, but measured the basket a second time. Much to his surprise, the basket was a half inch low (hence the reason for the missed shots).

The point of this story is to show you the importance of knowing exactly what the goal is that you're shooting for. Larry Bird's goal was a circle of metal attached to a glass backboard ten feet from the floor. Our goal as a Christian is to love others with a healthy heart, a clean conscience, and a flawless faith. We too, should know in our spirits when the goal is a bit off and we are probably missing our mark. To love others is not only to share Jesus with them, but to follow up with discipleship. In other words, you will be striving after this goal for the rest of your life so don't expect to stop anytime soon. Larry Bird didn't get all his recognition and rewards in the sport of basketball by missing his mark often. Christians likewise don't see the fruits of their labor by failing to follow through with specific instructions. Perfect practice makes perfect. Hey, and in the end, we'll all be all-stars in heaven!

GROW! How does this scripture apply to your daily life? What makes athletes good at what they do? How does that differ from what allows Christians to excel in their faith? Do you know your exact goals as a believer? Where are the measurements found? (Hint: the Bible)

READY, *"He raises the poor from the dust and lifts the needy from the ash heap; he seats them with princes and has them inherit a throne of honor." 2 Samuel 2:8*

SET, It was definitely a sight like I had never seen before. 'Box City' is a whole community of poverty stricken people living in cardboard boxes for shelter beneath the mix master of overpasses and interchanges just east of downtown Dallas. We're talking hundreds of families (moms, dads, kids, grandpas, etc.), assembled in rows like a trailer park, just trying to make it until the next day. Their occupations are beggars, trash diggers, can collectors, robbers, and thieves. Upon my visit, I was welcomed with open arms like a king at a banquet. This was definitely one scene in reality I won't soon forget.

Realize it or not, we are all poor in one way or another. Those who think that money is the measure of success suffer from a poverty of imagination and intellect. Some suffer a poverty of love, security, emotional stability, self-image, and self-value.

The Bible makes very clear the fact that the most alarming sort of poverty is spiritual. This type of poverty affects every race, class, nationality, age, and sex. The remedy for this sickness is offered by God through His Son Jesus on the Cross. Each of us show what we sincerely love by happily devoting our attention it. Go ahead, take a look around you and see if you don't see poverty in plenty. Don't look just at those in rags living in cardboard boxes. Look also at those in fancy cars, sporting fashionable clothes, and talking on cellular phones. Poverty comes in all shapes and sizes and sometimes dresses in 'camo' in order to not draw attention to itself (but in reality, those who are stricken are in big time need).

GROW! When you think of poverty what do you imagine? Do you see poverty in your school, home, or community? How do we help those who can't help themselves?

BAD HABITS

READY, *"Do you not know that your body is a temple for the Holy Spirit who is in you whom you have received from God?"* I Corinthians 6:19

SET, The 'he-man' rugged model for the macho nacho cigarette powerhouse, Marlboro, succumbed to cancer at age fifty-one. You may remember him as the weathered cowboy, marked with tattoos and chapped lips, who rode the range punching cows like the men of the old west. What he did for the manufacturer was lead consumers to believe the stud thing to do was to smoke. What we didn't see on the billboards was that he spent the last three years of his life warning others of the dangers of smoking. Though it was too late for him, he thought if he could keep just one youth from starting, or help one smoker to stop, it would all be worth it. He was a convincing spokesperson, because he knew all too well the price to be paid for becoming enslaved to this habit. You'll never see a magazine ad or billboard poster showing a smoke-filled room of emaciated hackers throwing up their offerings to the god of tobacco. The lesson can be learned that all of us can be overtaken by a habit which owns our lives and body.

My personal belief is that if God intended us to smoke we would all be born with exhaust systems. Granted, this is just one of many bad habits that we bow down to. We are to worship no other god than the Creator of the universe. Another god could be classified as anything that takes jurisdiction in our lives and fights for the number one spot in our hearts. Bad habits develop simply from lack of self-control. Take control of those areas that have escaped from the corral and are now running wild in your life. Seek help from other supporting believers by confessing the habit and the need for their prayers and accountability. Don't forget there is a big God who loves you and all He desires is to be asked for His help to make you more like His Son, then look out! Bad habits are like a comfortable couch, easy to get into, and hard to get out of.

GROW! What bad habits do you have that have taken over in your life? Do you desire to quit? Do you want to quit bad enough to seek help? When are you gonna' start?

READY, *"And Jesus answered them and said 'I Am He.' They drew back and fell to the ground." John 18:6*

SET, Unfortunately, some of the funniest commercials on the tube today are beer commercials. Bud Light aired an ad with a guy coming off a plane, walking up to three limo drivers holding signs with names, asking which one of the drivers had Bud Light in his limo. When one fessed up to having the requested item, the guy quickly looked at the sign and said, "Then I'm Doctor Gal-o-week-its." The limo driver abruptly asked this guy, "You're Doctor Galakowetz?" to which the impersonator answers very clearly "Yes, I am."

You know, when I first heard this commercial during a televised football game I recalled another person in the history of time answering the question with a similar "Yes I am He," but under different circumstances. Let's look back at the time that Jesus and Peter were confronted by an army of soldiers searching for Jesus to take Him to trial before the people and Pilot. I guess the commander came up to Jesus, asked if He was Jesus the Nazarene, and Jesus replied, "I Am He," and the entire army fell flat. God told Moses in Exodus 3:14, "I Am who I Am." In other words, there is only one 'I Am' and that is God, the creator of everything. There is so much power in those simple words, yet in this day and time so little respect for our Lord. We too should fall on our faces daily to praise and worship and give honor to the God who cared enough to incarnate in a flesh suit to save us. We shouldn't be messin' with the title of CEO of our world, God. Hey, one more thing...if you're gonna' be a light, *don't* be a Bud Light. That type of light flutters to a mere flicker quickly!

GROW! Why is the title *The Great I Am* so powerful? What does 'I Am' do for you? How can we be more reverent to our Lord and Creator?

OLD SELF

READY, *"Knowing this fact, that our old self was crucified with Christ and that our body of sin might be done away with and that we should no longer be slaves to sin." Romans 6:6*

SET, A few years ago a precious Godly lady came up to me one hot summer day and gave me a gold nugget of wisdom. We had been talking of our mutual struggles to keep ourselves above reproach, yet how tough it was to not slip back in our old ways. I was sharing how even though I had been crucified with Christ, I was amazed that the re-appearing of my old self was far too frequent. She reminded me that we as Christians were crucified, along with our old nature with Christ, but that in the days of the Roan deaths that the crucifixion that Jesus went through was the slowest form of death a person could go through. Death on the cross was not meant to be quick and simple. It was intended to be long-lasting and grueling.

Just as the apostle Paul writes, the old self has been put to death on the cross of Calgary with Christ, but it's also a daily ordeal, too. Yes, we as followers do only accept Christ in our hearts sincerely one time, yet we have to continually remember where we came from (sin nature). Our old sinful selfish self needs a good kick in the pants everyday in which we breath. You're always gonna' make mistakes, which is why we are saved by *grace*, not works. Our goal is not to be perfect, just pressin' on everyday of our lives to try to think, walk, talk, and act like our role model Jesus. Don't try to work on your weak areas from the outside in, but the inside (heart) out. Transformation is not a snap of the finger, wiggle of the nose, wave the magic wand occurrence...it's a process. Realize that daily God Gives you pop quizzes in your faith to let you see what areas you need to work on in His class. Set your sights high and your expectations attainable, and you will be on your way to a fulfilled life. Go for it!

GROW! What areas of your life do you see your old nature rear its evil head? How do you handle it? How can you handle it better next time?

READY, "Do all things without grumbling or disputing, that you may prove to be blameless and innocent, children of God above reproach in the midst of a crooked and perverse generation among whom you shine like starts in the universe." Philippians 2:14-15

SET, Have you ever thought of yourself as a star on another sort of stage? Well, you are! You're a shining star, and you're not even on the show *Star Search* (with old big mouth Ed Mac). Have you ever noticed that we live in one of the most arguing, finger pointing, foot stomping societies ever (just listen for a minute in a crowded mall)? Realize that to be negative or find the worst in every situation is the easy way. Did you know it takes like ten times the effort to frown as it does to smile? So why do we see folks daily that walk around with a look on their face like they smell something stinky?

Honestly, you don't have to do much to show just how different you are as a Christian. Try going a week in your house without arguing with your sibling, or smartin' off when you're asked to straighten up the room or take out the trash. Try saying 'yes sir' to your dad, or 'thank you' and 'please' more than once a century and see if you won't have to revive your parents who pass out from surprise. As a believer, we have continually got to keep on our toes to prove to a cynical world that we are blameless and innocent (not perfect) children of God who live an unaccused life for Jesus.

I'll end this devo with a word picture that will best show you how we are to appear to a lost generation. You are a star shining brightly against a back-drop of darkness who will stay shining until the 'Son' reappears back on earth to take His star children home to rest from their work. Wow...look out Ed McMahon, this is a real search for stars!

GROW! Do you do things without grumbling or arguing? Are you a joy or pain to live with? How can you be more blameless and shine to a world that lives in darkness daily?

T.G.I.F.

READY, "God demonstrated His own love for us, in that while we were still sinners, Christ died for us (you)." Romans 5:8

SET, We hear it all the time...T.G.I.F...thank God it's Friday! Most folks throw this term around like a monkey does a banana peel, and don't have a clue what it really means. Most use it without any reverence to or for God and they are just bustin' at the seams, because it signals the last of the workweek. It allows folks to go ballistic for two days each week when they can relax, play, take a nap, and basically just 'do their own thing.' The Friday before Easter, you know chocolate bunnies and sugar eggs, is called Good Friday. It's a day where millions of believers in Christ all over this planet are mindful of what God did for them through Christ, His Son, two thousand years previously. Why is it so good, when it marks a dreadful day when a blameless lamb was sent to slaughter on a cross at Calvary for you and me? That sure doesn't sound like my definition of good by any stretch of the imagination. Sounds more like a 'day that Jesus went down in defeat' than it does a day we should celebrate each year.

The apostle Paul gives us the answer in an nutshell. The love here is too profound for any Einstein to grasp, yet so simple that any little child could accept. No doubt, T.G.I.F. by all means. This truly is a day which sets the tone for a happy Easter and excitement to be worshipping a living (not dead) God. Next time you hear the disc jockey on the radio use that phrase, T.G.I.F., maybe you can be thankful of one particular Friday in history...it will bring more joy than finding some old hard-boiled egg I bet.

GROW! What is the significance in Good Friday to a Christian? What does Easter mean to you? How can this one Friday in history change someone's life? Why do other religion's worship a dead god? How cool is it that Jesus is alive today?

READY, *"Grandchildren are the crown of old men, and the glory of son's in their fathers."* Proverbs 17:6

SET, It's a shame what our society is doing to and with our elderly. The system throws off to the side, like an old pair of shoes, some of the wisest people on the planet. Yes, they may drive a bit slower than most or need additional volume when being addressed, but they are precious to our livelihood. We all, in due time and if we're lucky, will grow to be a ripe old age and be a grandparent someday. Sit down, if your grandparents are still alive, and take a few moments just tap into their past experiences and keen knowledge of this life we all seek to live abundantly. Do you realize how valuable you are or were to your grandparents? Read that scripture again, and this time, mix in a little perspective and heartfelt compassion. Do you see how it's worded? Do you catch the true intent of the real message? You *are* (or were) the *crown* of Grandma and Pa. God uses crowns to reward His children for a job well done. Grandparents view their children's children as a reward from the Lord which they desire to show off.

Let me ask you a straight forward question, do (or did) you respect, love and honor your grandparents? Do you value time with them like they value and cherish the time with you? I realize that time and geography hinder us at times on the visits, but hey, we do have the technology of the telephone and postcards. Just a simple note (not a novel) will do as an expression of your love and commitment. When people receive a note they see one thing, that you, wherever you are, took the time out of your rat race schedule to think of them and write something on a card, lick and stick a stamp, and mail it. Don't ever forget...life is just full of a lot of little things stacked up. Make today a day when you can honor your grandparents and show them that they too, are a crown of honor.

GROW! When was the last time you told your grandparents you love them? Why or why not? How can you better cultivate that relationship today? Will you? (You better!)

READY, *"Therefore what God has joined together let no man separate." Matthew 19:6*

SET, We're in the age of technology and descriptive words, so we have changed a bit. Years ago if your parents got a divorce it was called 'growing up in a broken home,' but now in the more hip lingo we call it 'coming from a dysfunctional family.' Call it what you want, but six out of every ten people who read this devo come from a 'whatever' family such as mine. I remember twenty years ago being looked at by others as some sort of pitiful freak of hard luck. Divorce today is not as harshly looked upon and, in fact, is becoming more common than weddings. I could rattle out a list of statistics that would raise the hair on your back, but I think you're all too aware of the dangers. Most of you reading this book have dreams of getting married, buying a home surrounded by a white picket fence, on a one acre lot with a stream running through it, having a mess of children playing games on the green front lawn while you and your spouse grin from ear to ear on the front porch swing. If it only was as easy as it appears.

The minor prophet Malachi gives God's verdict on divorce... "I hate it" (Malachi 2:16). Many folks today think this is too rigid or harsh, but the covenant made between a man and woman must be taken with seriousness. Jesus talks of divorce in the Sermon on the Mount and echoes this opinion. Not everyone is going to be called into the bond of marriage, but if you are, realize that a marriage for life is *not* built on the wedding ceremony, but the vows. I personally feel there is too much emphasis placed on all the hoop-la of the building, tuxedo and dress styles, catering, special singers, and get-away car, than listening to the vows repeated. Don't get me wrong now, the ceremonies aren't bad as long as they are the start of a life-long covenant to Christ and each other. Coming from a person who saw and went through the divorce of parents, do yourself and God a big favor by marrying for life or don't marry at all.

GROW! Why are we called to marry for life? What kind of witness is it to be faithful to God and your spouse? Are you willing to be different?

No Guts, No Glory

READY, *"The proof of your faith, being more precious than gold which is perishable, even though tested by fire, may be found to result in praise, glory and honor to Christ." 1 Peter 1:7*

SET, Close your eyes (no dozing off now) and say to yourself the title of this devo and see what visions dance in your head. No fair seeing sugar plums either. This kind of line is called 'baiting' if you want to know the street name for it. You use this 'one-liner' when you want to coax, or persuade, someone to do something they probably wouldn't do on their own will. It's kind of a 'guts' check on the spot, you might say. You'll hear it on the ski slopes, on the twenty foot bluffs of a lake, in the athletic arenas, and at the late night parties. Sometimes it's a sincere effort to motivate, and other times it's to get someone up for failure or destruction. No matter where you call home, or what your age is, this phrase chooses no favorites and knows not of the consequences.

You hear this lingo in the secular world more than you will in the Christian circles. I offer you a suggestion. We need to hear it more on the God Squad too. Isn't it true we are athletes, warriors, risk takers, in this forgiven family? Are we not called to run in such a way that we may *win*!? Doesn't it take guts to receive the crown of eternal life called heaven? You bet your sweet potatoes it does! This Christian stuff is no walk through the lily fields or a yellow brick road (sorry Dorothy). Folks without guts in this league (Christianity) won't last too long. I would much rather be considered a risk taker in my faith, than a bench sitter. It's a heck of a lot better to have tried and failed, than never to have tried at all. Failure helps us realize that we are human and we *do* need a Savior. Step up to the plate and take a hundred percent swing. Remember, home runs in this league are always preceded by a few strike outs, but that makes the successes for Christ all the more to celebrate about. Have some guts and see some glory. Go God's way.

GROW! Why do you shy away from uncertain situations in your faith? How can you have God's guts?

READY, *"Listen to advice and accept instruction and in the end you will be wise." Proverbs 19:20*

SET, He had run with some of the roughest, toughest, outlaws to ever show up on the wild west scene. His area of expertise was his capability to crack the toughest bank vaults without ever laying a finger on them. You didn't read about him in your history books or see his story brought to life on the silver screen. His name was Tanner Watson, and he was blind at birth. He ran with Jesse James and 'Wild Bill' Hickock. Their victims were towns like Tombstone, Abilene, Dodge City, and Deadwood. They had to fight off Indians led by Sitting Bull and Crazy Horse along with cattle thieves out of the Mexican badlands south of Texas. The heyday of this historical cowboy lasted from 1867 to 1887, and life wasn't as glamorous or as romantically dangerous as it has been portrayed by the movies. Tanner survived those days to become the master of safe crackers. Because of his incredible ability to 'listen' to the flaws in locks, he could pick them or figure out their combination in just a few turns of the dial. He would pull up a chair in front of the vault and have one of the outlaws spin the lock's dial until told to stop and write down the specific number they stopped on. This process was done day after day, bank after bank.

This old west character had a gift that we can utilize in a little more positive, productive, and much less dangerous way. The following techniques are a few ways in which you can increase your effectiveness in the art of listening:

Maintain eye contact.

Always sit or stand facing your partner.

Concentrate on what's being said.

Avoid distractions such as constant movement.

Use facial responses (nod) to show you're listening.

Ask relevant questions.

Re-state what your partner said to assure correct interpretation.

God has given each of us the capability of listening. Listening to someone translates into 'you care.' Be a collector of the tools for the art of listening.

GROW! How well do you listen? What makes listening so hard? Why are there so few good listeners?

A Promise To Restore

READY, *Then I will make up to you for the years that the swarming locusts have eaten." Joel 2:25*

SET, The prophet Joel is writing this truth to the southern kingdom of Judah. He reminds them of the historical judgment of the Lord and warns of future judgment. He exhorts them to "rend your heart and not your garments." Judah had experienced a terrible plague of locusts which destroyed the vegetation of their land. This land was desolate.

My heart can feel that same desolation emotionally if I focus on my years of not knowing Jesus, living contrary to God's commandments, and doing nothing with eternal significance. Because of the choices I made in my early twenties, I can easily jump into the sin of self-protection of my heart.

I claim and cling to this promise from my God to me. He promises to restore to me all of those lost fruits of wasted years of living in disobedience. As I increasingly become aware of the reality of His forgiveness and the way He presently views me, I do walk in that restoration. I do begin to feel again, to want to love again. Joel 2:26 says, "And you shall have plenty to eat and be satisfied; and praise the name of the Lord your God, who has dealt wondrously with you, Then my people will never be put to shame." My heart is overwhelmingly grateful to Jesus for making it possible for me to walk in satisfaction and without shame about who I am. All of this only because of the blood of Jesus.

This promise reminds me that God is not concerned with who I was in the past, but who I am becoming right now. It reminds me of God's grace and desire for me to have an abundant life now! Every day He does move me closer to a point of being able to love people with a reckless abandonment and truly receive and experience love in return.

GROW! Do you feel at times robbed of a future? What is the difference in the old law and new one in Christ? What made it possible to restore our hope? How can you really believe?

WHAT IF?

READY, *"Now to the King eternal, immortal, invisible, the only God, be honor and glory forever."* 1 Timothy 1:17

SET, Let's play the 'what if' game for a minute. What if you could make yourself invisible for one day? What sort of things would you do, and where would you want to go? Okay, since you didn't answer quick enough, I will. If I were invisible for just one day of my life, I'd do things like:

> *Hang out at the water fountain and turn it up full blast when some one leaned over to drink.*
> *Go to a library and play tricks on the librarian.*
> *Pull up to a McDonald's drive-through window in a car (with no driver) and order fries.*
> *Push the ball off the tee during kick-off at a televised football game.*
> *Go to the zoo and mess with the gorillas in the cages.*
> *Change the channel on the TV when my dad was watching golf.*
> *Scream in church (I'm warped).*
> *Trip a thief making his getaway.*
> *Help a kid learning to ride a bike by holding him up to keep from crashing.*
> *Clean up litter without anyone knowing.*

Believe it or not, we worship a living God who is omnipresent (everywhere at once). Did you know that one of many differences in Satan and God is that God can be everywhere at the same time, but Satan can only be in one place at a time (demons make up for his shortcomings)? It is so reassuring to know that when I drive, fly, walk, or run that I can talk to the Creator local, not long distance. With this invisible quality we have a guarantee He's there. How? Just like the wind, you can't see but can feel and know its power. The sheer fact that Jesus is so nearby gives me the luxury of calling upon him at a moments notice and not having to wait for a response time. Next time you're in your car, jogging, playing sports, walking to class, working, and trying to talk (praying) to Him with your eyes open in your heart, trust me, God will still hear you even if you're not on your knees, eyes closed. We are able to pray unceasingly (1 Thessalonians 5:17). Now what would you do if you *were* invisible for a day? Have fun dreamin.'

GROW! Why do you think God chose to be invisible? What security do you have knowing He's always there?

READY, *"By this all men will know you are My disciples if you have love for one another." John 13:35*

SET, One of the greatest movies to hit the screen in a long time was Hoosiers. Granted, I am an old basketball player, so it's no surprise it appealed to me. The story was of a small farming town, in who-knows-where Indiana, which had a small school with a new coach (Gene Hackman). No one wanted, nor could they take the time away from plowing, to try out for this team of renegades. The suspense begins to build as the peon team begins to win and ultimately makes its way to the big time state championships in Indianapolis. During the final game they began to get thumped on by this big city team being led by a star post man. The head coach pulls his player aside and tells him to guard this big-time player so close that he will be able to tell the coach what flavor gum he's chewing. A few minutes on the clock passes and the small town team starts their comeback and the player runs by the bench and yells, "Hey Coach...it's spearmint." The coach just grins and nods his head with pride.

We all need to take on that coaching strategy as we get to know other believers. We need to get so closely knit and united in spirit that we can tell someone what the other person's likes, dislikes, goals, and dreams are. The only way to get to know someone in an intimate, deep-level capacity is through spending t-i-m-e. Friendships are no different than stocks, bonds, and retirement funds. They are all an investment in your future. What "time" translates into is sacrifice, and sacrifice translates into dedication, and dedication into loyalty, and so on. You can clearly see that loving someone unconditionally is not a one-time thing...it's a process we all grow into with God and time. The young player's reward for getting so close to the other player was a championship...for you, companionship.

GROW! What does loyalty mean to you? How could you really get close to a fellow believer today? Is it worth it to you? When are you gonna' start? Today?

READY, "Let us not become weary in doing good, for at the proper time we will reap a harvest if we don't give up." Galatians 6:9

SET, It was tagged as being one of the most powerful messages ever spoken to an audience and yet only took two seconds to deliver and consisted of only four words. Winston Churchill was the giver during the war and Great Britain was the receiver. It went something like this, "Never, never, never quit." The End. Wow...what a masterpiece, right? I mean, come on, how long did it take him to memorize this? I wonder who wrote his speeches, a second grader? It may have been simple, but like my old coach use to say, "K.I.S.S. Keep It Simple, Stupid." There might not have been much, but it communicated a much needed point. Locker rooms nationwide are full of one-liner quotes like "to quit is to lose," or "Quitters never win and winners never quit." The six phases to most projects are 1) enthusiasm, 2) disillusionment, 3) panic, 4) search for the guilty, 5) punishment of the innocent, and 6) praise to the new participant(s).

You know people are so conditioned to 'get out' if the heat (pressure) gets too tough that we bale out of marriages, relationships, jobs, school, practice, and projects. It is consoling to know that Jesus didn't take on a quitter's mentality and give up on the cross. There is tons of reading available on the start of a process, but not on the middle or finish of one. To maintain a steady pace throughout the course is a tough row to hoe. You've got to have a Jesus mind set and God's heart to do so. What we need in our communities, families, and occupations today are those few and far between breeds of believers who dare the odds to win at all cost. Be one of those endangered species and see what a difference you'll make for the furthering of the Kingdom. Quitting is like a comfortable bed...easy to get into and hard to get out of.

GROW! What situations arise in your life that cause you to want to give up? Are you developing a bad habit of quitting? How can you *not* become a consistent quitter?

Don't Look Now

READY, *"Be strong and very courageous. Be careful to obey all the laws my servant Moses gave you; don't look to the right or left so you may be successful in all you do." Joshua 1:7*

SET, If you would like to know a highlight of my life, it was teaching and watching my son learn to ride a bike for the first time. You remember...Don't look down, sit up tall, pedal fast, lean into turns, watch for trees, and don't scream when you fall. Most parents hold the back of the seat when they are teaching (I held the back of my son's neck) the balance process. I must have run ten miles chasing behind the little man, in fear of the first wipe-out. I remembered one thing my dad told me that helped, and I echoed it to my boy, "Don't look to the right or left, keep your eyes forward at all times." The purpose of those words of wisdom was to prevent a face plant in the pavement.

After Moses' death at the banks of the flooded River Jordan where a pupil named Joshua was to take over leading about three million whiny Israelites to freedom, you'll find a gold nugget that applies today. Joshua receives from God Himself, a formula from the Father of Freedom. God tells Josh (we'll call him that for short...best friends we were) to be strong and courageous, knowing he had it in him, and not to be scared. Why not? Josh wasn't exactly an expert in piloting people to the land God had promised was theirs to take. He tells Josh to be obedient to the instructions (which happen to be the Ten Commandments), and then comes the one-two punch...don't look to the right or left so you will be successful wherever you go and whatever you do. I wonder if that advice came from my dad? (Kidding!) To put it in our loose-lipped lingo, God is telling him to focus on the goal and go for it. Be like a sprinter that stares at the finish tape, not the boy in the grandstands selling popcorn. Who knows, this advice could come in handy for you someday.

GROW! How important is it that you focus in on your goal? What distracts you to your right or left? How can you prevent it?

SNAIL OR CROCODILE

READY, *"Avoid worthless and empty chatter because it leads others to ungodliness and their talk will spread like gangrene."* 2 Timothy 2:16-17

SET, Growing up, I bet you had some pets around your house. I would wager to say that one pet you never had was a snail. Now I'm not referring to a slug, because there is a major difference (and not that one melts with salt and the other one doesn't). Believe it or not, the little crawling creature has teeth on its tongue. That's right. Scientists have examined the tongue of a snail (they must have been bored) and found that the microscope revealed as many as thirty thousand little teeth. It keeps its tongue coiled up in its mouth like a roll of toilet paper until it's needed. Then it shoots that dude out uses it like a chain saw on leaves and stems. Wow! You've learned some trivia about the snail, so don't hesitate to enlighten others during a dinner conversation, okay?

You're gonna' say this is one lame similarity but we too use our tongue like the snail. We walk around with this muscle next to our molars and lash out for the purpose (at times) of sawing down people or reputations. We talk about things that are empty and basically useless to even bring up and we tear down more than we build up. What I call 'tainted talk' eventually ends up producing a gangrene that will only be cured by amputation. We would do better to pattern our life after a crocodile. Why? Because a croc' has powerful jaws, large sharp teeth, and lips, but no tongue. Be careful what and who you talk about and shall we say "Tis better to be a crocodile than a snail." (Okay...so the ending is kinda' weak).

GROW! What sort of things do you talk about with your friends? Are you more like a snail or crocodile? Do you see how empty chatter leads others into sin? How can you avoid that?

READY, *"He will stand and shepherd his flock in the strength of the Lord, in the majesty of the name of the Lord his God. And they will live securely, for then his greatness will reach to the ends of the earth. And He will be their peace." Micah 5:4-5*

SET, Since George Washington's first inauguration in April of 1789 through Bill Clinton's reign, we have had wars and rumors of wars to live with. For the past two hundred years of America's history, we have survived World War I and II, Korea, Vietnam, and most recently the Gulf War. The war that seems to have left its mark in our history books is the Civil War era. It was four years of vicious, devastating warfare that cost hundreds of thousands of lives, divided families and friends, and left half the country smoldering. The war was between the North's commercial economic structure (railroads, canals, steamships, etc.) and the South's agrarian slave-based economy which provided cotton, tobacco, rice, and corn. The simplest explanation for the war might be that the southerners didn't want to be told how to live their lives. The struggle for control was a powder keg with a long burning fuse which ultimately exploded with horrifying results which we still see today.

As long as we all live on the same planet, there will be rumors of war. Where you have people, you have a difference in philosophies, ideas, and ways of doing things. Everyone always thinks their way is best and hold the mentality 'my way or the highway.' Take a look back since the division of Cain and Abel and you'll see two paths, two ways. We all are looking for that plot of peace to seek shelter and refuge in, a quiet spot which is secure for ourselves and our families removed from the violence and destruction. Let me tell you that the only *peace* you'll ever have in this lifetime is with our Lord. He is the producer of peace, Savior of security and the refuge of redemption. He *will stand* between us and an angry world. He *will* fill the gap of peace and war, and finally, He *will* return to take us to that shelter in the sky we call Heaven. He is the Prince of Peace, you know.

GROW! If Webster's dictionary called you to define peace, what would you tell them? Where do you seek peace? Why do we want peace so bad?

PODS

READY, *"If any widow has children, let them learn to practice piety in regard to their own family, and make some return to their parents for this is good in God's eyes." 1 Timothy 5:4*

SET, Recently, I was watching one of those educational shows which come on late Sunday evenings. This particular show was a documentary on those zany creatures of the sea (no, not the Little Mermaid), the killer whale. These enormous conglomerations of blubber, fins, and teeth have intrigued me since I visited Sea World in Florida and got spit on by Shamu. I did learn though, that these predators of the sea seem to have the personality of a puppy and the family standards we ought to have. Their family is correctly called a 'pod' and they stay together at all times. Starting at the moment of birth, the calf (baby whale) and its mommy will always breath in unison...the mom surfaces for air at the same time as her young. The families of whales can be as large as fifty, and stay together until death. They hunt, swim, play, and learn from each other throughout their life-span. So, the next time you see one at an aquarium, look past the flips and stunts, and notice the loyalty that runs deeper than any ocean.

We've lost the art of 'pod' making. In human terms, we don't value the family unit like we should and God intended. Our number one focus here on earth is to build a structure (like the three little pigs) that can't be blown down by the wolves of time. Alcohol, divorce, drugs, anger, rebellion, and sex outside marriage are a few weapons of wind the wolves huff and puff to try to blow down our homes. To change the trends we have got to put a huge value on the family fortress and never give in to the armies of hell. Satan would like nothing more than to destroy our lives through a dysfunctional family. A family needs to be a refuge, haven, security blanket, and living quarters of love, therein serving its' chosen purpose. We need to take a lesson from the untainted lifestyle of the killer whales of the sea and get our family back swimming together. Realize that Christ is and will have to be the glue which holds your pod together. Begin by eating one meal a day, praying one time a day, serving once a week, and encouraging once an hour.

GROW! What is your definition of a family? Does it jive with the biblical one? Are you glue in your home? How?

A COSTLY DECISION

READY, *"So because you are lukewarm, neither hot nor cold, I will spit you out of My mouth." Revelation 3:16*

SET, Of all the sports to choose from on the smorgasbord of athletics, biking is definitely one of them. I don't say that with a tone of sarcasm in my pen, but let's say it's from the view point of someone who learned from the school of hard falls. One of my monumental moments in motion, was to race my best friend down the biggest hill (if you could call it that) in Dallas at the age of ten. You might be asking yourself, "Self, how can this be so tough?" Well, include the ingredient of a squirrel, and you'll get the picture. I had a three-speed Schwinn with a banana seat and my friend had a new Huffy with a horn. He continually bragged about his ride on rims to the point that I thought he (and it) needed a taste of humble pie. We were riding home from school when the challenge was issued, and he took it like a dog to a bone. The hill was about one block long. No cars were in site, so we put the pedals to the metal and let 'em go. About half way through the race a squirrel ran out in front of me and continued running as fast as one-inch legs can go. It went right, left, right, then decided to stop right smack in the path of my front tire. I couldn't tell what the wacko creature was thinking, but didn't want to hit it, so I turned a hard left, hit the curb and flipped into a neighbor's sticker bush. The squirrel smiled at the site, then climbed a tree without one ounce of remorse.

Daily, we are faced with decisions of direction in our lives. We sometimes don't have any direction, so we go back and forth and cause chaos along the way for ourselves, and others. You make your decisions, then your decisions will make you. Being a lukewarm Christian doesn't appeal to Christ at all. Do you see what He compares that to? Spit. Those who stand in the middle of the street get run over by traffic both ways. Do yourself, and the entire Christian army, a favor, and be hot for Jesus. Make your move and stand strong with it. Don't cause the folks who are riding behind you (non-Christians) to wreck their lives on the curb of compromise.

GROW! Are you hot or cold for Christ? When do you decide wrong?

READY, *"This is the word of the Lord 'not by might nor by power but by My spirit' says the Lord." Zechariah 4:6*

SET, You've probably seen the T-shirts that say 'Big team little me' or 'I is in the middle of sin.' They are usually advertised by different teams to express their motto for the upcoming season. We, the people of America, are rich in talent and twist. Look around you, and you'll see a wealth of resources, technology, military capabilities, leadership qualities, agricultural production, economic stamina and creativity. The people of this great nation do a heck of a lot just on sheer raw talent and gifts. I dare say that the great things accomplished have been empowered by God but credit goes to self. If you listen real close to conversation going on around you, you'll hear the work 'I' used more often than 'us' or 'we.' We produce faster than Detroit does cars, an environment that structurally seems to cultivate an independent mentality and way of thinking.

You will never understand the true meaning of teamwork until you join forces with the Creator of Accomplishments. Come on, I mean, how many individuals do you know who went into their office, workshop, or meeting rooms and came out with an entire universe stacked with creatures. God knows you have talents and what they are because He gave them to you. You did nothing to earn them and He sure didn't owe you them. True joy in an accomplishment is giving the credit to what and who the credit is due. if you think you pulled your own self up by the boot straps, I got news for ya.' God put those boots on you to begin with. He is the Master Mechanic that fine tunes us daily to be the fuel efficient, motorized mortal we were meant to be. Before you start out after a goal like a bluetick hound chasing a coon, stop and ask God to guide and direct your every move and step along the way, so that you'll begin to be a winner by His Spirit, not your flesh.

GROW! Ask a friend how often you use the word *I*. How much do you do *without* God? How can you start doing things with God?

SOLID AS THE ROCK

READY, *"Be to me a rock of habitation to which I may continually go; Thou hast given commandment to save me for You are my rock and my fortress." Psalm 71:3*

SET, A sailor in a violent shipwreck was thrown overboard and onto a rock in the sea where he clung for his life throughout the dark, stormy night alone. Later on, while being rescued by the Coast Guard, a crew member asked, "Didn't you shake and tremble with fear for your life when you were clinging to that rock?" The sailor replied, "Yes, I did...but the rock didn't."

Today, hearing the word 'rock' may bring thoughts of dancing, a particular band, style of music, a boulder or cliff, or the motion of an unstable object. We may think of a rugged, unfeeling type of a person. The 'rock' I'm referring to is the "Rock of Ages, cleft for me, let me hide myself in thee." This is The Rock who doesn't roll, and, who doesn't even budge with a blast. The old hymn, which is the third most widely known and sung hymn in our Christian heritage seems to sum up what Jesus is to us. When we are cast into the turbulent water of time, He is all we can hold on to.

We seem to be living in an exercise oriented society which has begun to love to explore its limits with climbing and rappelling rocks. Why so? For the feeling of accomplishment and challenge? For the extremes of the elements? For the rush of a three hundred foot rappel or a one thousand foot north face climb? I believe we, as a people, are fascinated with rocks, because of their unique beauty and strength. Whether you're a geologist, climber, bulldozer operator, dynamite specialist, or collector, rocks are interesting. Our God is an awesome God, and He alone is the rock of our salvation and the foundation on which we build our lives. He is the fortress that we hide behind and the matter in which we cling in stormy seas. Whichever picture shows up in your head when you think of a rock, there are none so big, sturdy, awesome, and available as God our Father. Study Him, collect His thoughts, cleave to His commandments, and hold to His holiness because this Rock don't roll.

GROW! What is the rock you cling to? Why are we told to grow and build our lives on Him? What security do you have hugging this rock in turbulent times?

CROSS EXAMINATION

READY, *"You who are going to destroy the temple and rebuild it in three days, save Yourself! If you are the Son of God come down off that cross." Matthew 27:40*

SET, If you've never seen it on TV, you surely have seen this rush hour of rhetoric take place on the evening news. It's a dueling tongue tango between two attorneys (that's a tongue twister if I've ever seen one) which takes place daily across this country. The arena is a big courtroom, the referee is the judge (the dude in the black robe with a mallet), the coaches are the lawyers (dressed in starch), the player is the accused (scared spit-less), and the onlookers are the jurors (the ones summoned to do this). The prosecutor and the defender are going at it, like two cats after the same mouse, politicizing to win the votes of the jurors. They call on witnesses and testimonies of folks and begin to cross-examine them to shreds. What takes place during a cross examination is that a witness is called to the stand by the opposing party for the purpose of testing the reliability of his previous testimony. Boy howdy, that's when all the prior law school know-how comes in to play and things get ugly.

Read the verse above again...I'll wait for ya.' Okay, did you see it or even hear it from the mouthy mockers? They were cross examining Jesus right there. Those worthless chumps were checking out the reliability of Jesus' previous statement. The problem is that they didn't or couldn't see the tree cuz' of the forest. What they should have been doing instead of a cross examination is an examination of the cross...get it? They didn't see what was happening right in front of their flappin' lips. They didn't realize the most important trial in history had taken place, and the jury found Jesus guilty of nothing but fulfilling prophecy. I would have to say that the scene in this courtroom was not, and never will be, re-enacted in any court of law again. Gahl-Lee, aren't you glad Jesus didn't decide to come down off that cross and commence kickin' some tail? That was what I'd have done but then again that's exactly why I'm not the Savior and Jesus is. He can handle the toughest cross examination to this day.

GROW! Do you daily cross examine God or examine the cross? Why not? How can you begin today? Will you?

READY, "*I press on toward the goal for the prize of the upward call of God in Christ Jesus.*" *Philippians 3:14*

SET, Okay, repeat this catchy rhythmic saying with me... "In fourteen hundred and ninety-two, Columbus sailed the ocean blue." A national holiday and two centuries of school books have taught us that Christopher Columbus, the great sailor and man of God (his name means Christ-bearer) reached America first, thus disproving the notion the world was flat. Americans celebrate this day of discovery on Columbus Day to stress the importance of the voyage and his incredible heroism and tenacity of character his quest must have demanded. Even the astronauts who flew to the moon had a pretty good idea of what at least to expect. Columbus was sailing, as *Star Trek* would put it, "where no man has gone before." After trying to sell his plan to the kings of Portugal, England, and France, he returned again to Isabella and Ferdinand of Spain for one last shot. Columbus showed them that the risks were small and the potential return great, and reminded them of the chance to stumble onto gold. The Spanish monarchs agreed to his consent. Columbus set sail on August 3, 1492 from Palos, Spain with three ships...Nina, Pinta, and the Santa Maria. On October 12 at 2:00 a.m. right before his crew of sailors were about to mutiny and force a return to Spain, a look-out named Rodrigo, aboard the Pinta, sighted 'land' by the light of the moon.

This is an incredible story of history in which a man of God has a goal and bars nothing to achieve it. To have the 'stick-with-it' mentality and a heart that never says die are two incredible qualities to bear. We can learn much from our past history and those who shaped and molded it. To have lived in 1492 without all the navigational devices or know how of computers to guide you across seas is remarkable. All they had were God-given smarts and a passionate desire to discover all that the Creator has to offer. How good are you at taking a vision or idea and following through with it 'til its completion? Determine what your goals in life are and get after it with God. Don't forget the old saying,."If you don't know what target you're shooting at, you'll probably hit it."

GROW! What is your goal today? How do goals help you get things accomplished in life and for God?

Whole Lot Of Shakin' Goin' On

READY, *"You are the salt of the earth; but if the salt has become tasteless, how will it be made salty again? It's good for nothing except to be thrown out and trampled under foot my men." Matthew 5:13*

SET, You may have been called a lot of things before (some too afflicted to mention) but how about this one....salt?. Jesus is telling you that you alone are the salt of the earth. Have you ever thought about what salt is used for? Besides seasoning, two others come to mind, first as a preservative, and second, to create thirst. Now, those are the most obvious reasons, but what's this about becoming tasteless? Have you ever tasted tasteless salt before? To have tasteless salt, you must first remove the key ingredient which is sodium (for all you inquiring minds that want to know). In ancient times the people would mix salt and a bitter substance called gypsum to create a putty type material which was used for patching roofs and walls in middle east homes. Whether you've been there or just seen in on the nightly news, you've noticed the homes in the far east all have flat roofs. These homes were designed that way to double as a roof and as a patio for entertaining guests at parties. When a hole was punched through on the roof (floor) it would be patch with the salt/gypsum putty and hence "trampled under the foot of men." The salt lost its taste because it was mixed with bitterness and lost its original purpose, so couldn't be made salty again.

You live as salt, someone who prevents the decay of society and creates a thirst for Christ, and if you mix with the bitter ritual and lifestyles of our civilization, you will become tasteless. You alone can help prohibit the decay in our families, schools, and among friends by shakin' a little salt on 'em. You can lead someone to Jesus by stimulating a thirst derived from the different lifestyle you lead. Don't forget that salt isn't worth much unless it's out of its shaker. Your church, youth group, clique of Christian friends isn't as valuable unless you go into our lost world and let them taste. As the saying goes, "you can lead a horse (a non-Christian) to water, but you can't make him drink (from the living water of Christ)," but you *can* if you put salt in his oats.

GROW! Who do you salt daily? Do you take the initiative? How can you prevent decay in our world today?

READY, "*Yes, woe upon you, Pharisees, and you other religious leaders—hypocrites! For you tithe down to the last mint leaf in your garden, but ignore the important things—justice and mercy and faith. Yes, you should tithe, but you shouldn't leave the more important things undone....You strain out a gnat and swallow a camel.*" Matthew 23: 23-24*

SET, As a child on my grandparents' farm, I spent time 'putting by' (as the farm folks say). 'Putting by' means preserving farm produce so it can be stored to use later. The method of the day was canning. My grandma was *good* at it. She canned everything, but my favorite was *jelly.*

We were so proud of the jelly we entered it in the fair one year, sure the judges would agree it was worth the effort it took to produce. But victory was not ours. A piece of peel had made it through the strainer and got wedged between the judge's teeth, so the prize went to someone who had made jelly from *commercial* grape juice, smooth and peel-less, but not 'homemade.'

Often in life we struggle so with insignificant (in the context of eternity) blips that we completely miss the genuine intent, then turn our backs and let a humongous injustice stomp right past us. Just prior to this verse Jesus spoke to the crowds concerning Jewish law in Jerusalem, after He'd booted the money changers out of the Temple. Angry at His acceptance from the crowd, the Pharisees tried to trip up Jesus with trick questions about *God's* laws.

If we're constantly searching for the smallest flaw, the least mistake, the one place where we colored outside the lines, we're liable to miss the grand design, the *big picture* (catchin' on?). Jesus said that if you follow the first and greatest commandment to love the Lord your God with all your heart, soul, and mind, you'll find you are obeying all the others (Matthew 23:37-40). Keep Jesus in your heart, your eyes on God, and don't sweat the small stuff. Gnats go down a lot easier than camels...one hump, or two?

GROW! What chokes you that really is insignificant in the light of eternity? Why?

LANDING LEADERS

READY, *"Let not many of you be leaders, because you know that we who lead will be judged more strictly." James 3:1*

SET, Flight #401 on Eastern Airlines was making a routine approach at the Lost Angeles airport. Throughout the journey there had been little or no turbulence and preparations were being made for landing. The crew was made up of five stewardesses, a captain, first assistant, and a flight navigator. After making final contact with the tower in L.A. and being cleared for landing, the captain flipped the switch to engage the landing gear, and noticed that the indicator light didn't come on. The crew did a quick visual check and found the landing gear was down which indicated that the light itself must be burned out. To make sure that the bulb was the problem, the plane continued to circle the airport while the navigator tried to remove the bulb from the instrument panel, but couldn't. The first assistant also tried, then the captain. Little did they realize that while the entire cabin crew was messing with one little bulb, the plane was losing altitude and ultimately crashed in a swampy area miles from the airport, killing hundreds. This tragedy was caused by a bulb valued at seventy-five cents. That's right...a cheap bulb was the root cause of a multi-million dollar plane and hundreds of lives. Why? Because the captain took his eyes off the big picture, his main responsibility, to deal with a meaningless job of no value.

We as leaders, need to keep flying the plane, not dabbling with dinkies. As a leader you must maintain a focus on what really matters or what doesn't at the time of decision making. We need to learn to 'choose our mountains' to climb in life. There is always gonna' be tons of stuff to do, events to volunteer for, committees to serve on, and meetings to attend, but there is really only twenty-four hours in a day (that I can tell). Learn to see (through God's eyes) what is a priority and what can wait. Learn to say no to some things and guard your time with your family and God. Learn to delegate to others so they can learn and you just take the priority lists. Leadership isn't a title, it's a learned skill.

GROW! Who is the best Christian leader you've ever seen at work? What made them so good at leading others? How can you be an effective leader? How do you learn to prioritize?

READY, *"For where your treasure is, there will your heart be also."*
Matthew 6:21

SET, A farmer, soon before his death, wanted to tell his sons of a secret. He gathered the boys up and said "Boys, I am soon to die of old age. I wanted to tell you of a hidden treasure that lies in the vineyard. Dig, and you will find it." Soon after, the father did pass away and so the sons took a couple of shovels and other gardening tools and began to dig. They turned the soil in the vineyard over and over, yet found no buried treasure. What they did find was that because of all the digging and loosening of the soil, the vines produced abundantly and yielded a record breaking crop like none had ever seen before. The moral of the story is...there is no treasure without toil.

We all seem to be looking for that buried treasure throughout our lives. We want to live out those fantasies we see on all those Disney pirate movies. Little do we all realize that what we really treasure is what we talk of the most. In other words, all you have to do to find out what someone really treasures is listen to them for a while. We treasure various things like people, places, things, moments, memories, feelings, etc. God wants, and is literally jealous of our hearts, and desires us to treasure our relationship with Him. Don't forget though, just like the moral to the story, there will be no treasure without the accompanying labor. You don't ever just stumble upon your treasure like the movies portray, you'll have to inject a little time and toil. You're not limited to only one treasure chest either, just make sure that the most valued one is your relationship with your Savior in shining armor. I'm sure that when you uncover the hidden treasure chest and open it up you'll find *your* heart there also.

GROW! What do you treasure most in your life? What treasures have a way of coming between you and God? Why? What can you do to keep your heart in the right treasure chest? Why does work always shadow true fulfillment in our lives?

What It Is Not Who It Is

READY, *"Hate what is evil...cling to what's good." Romans 12:9*

SET, *"All that is necessary for evil to prevail is for good men to do nothing."* Don't pass by this nugget of scripture like a pair of cheap sunglasses...look again. Do you see totally contradictory words in the same verse? Call it what you want, detest, despise, abhor, loathe, abominate, but it means what it says. You are to *hate* what is evil in this world and cling to what is good and right like a life buoy. Notice that it says 'what is' and not 'who is.' We are to hate the sin but not the sinner. Don't throw the baby out with the bath water kind of mentality. We live in this world but we don't have to be a part of it. Take a moment to remember all the things you hate to do or eat. How about broccoli or asparagus or hominy? How about taking out the trash, making your bed, doing homework, or practicing for a recital? The things you hate in life are the same vantage points you are to view all that is evil in our world today. Realize too that the world will probably hate you because it hated Jesus first.

We are to hate the evil and violence aired nightly on prime time TV. We are to loathe what ungodly shows are shown on the big screens across this country of ours in the theaters every Friday night. We should detest the gang murders we read about on our local front page newspapers. We are to abhor what goes on behind the walls of abortion clinics every second of the day. What can little old you do though? Love what is good, take a stand for what is right, pray for those who persecute you, be a light in a dark world for the cause of Christ and your voice *will* be heard and your life will be seen.

GROW! What kinds of things do you hate? What sort of things do you love? How can you apply this scripture in a non-violent, tasteful way today? Will it matter? (hint: yes!)

STOOPING

READY, *"But God demonstrates his own love for us in this: while we were yet sinners, Christ died for us." Romans 5:8*

"And being found in appearance as a man, he humbled himself and became obedient to death, even death on a cross!" Philippians 2:8

SET, There is a vivid picture in my brain of a ritual which seems to take place annually in March. If you know anything about horses or horse breeding, you know that March is the 'foal' time of the year. That's the time when pregnant mares have their colts out in pastures on ranches across the south. There is nothing quite like seeing a new-born colt trying with all its four-legged might to stand up and walk for the first time. It's amazing how soon after birth and the mom licking the colt clean that it learns to maneuver. I remember my dad, upon sight of a new-born colt in one of his pastures, crawling for up to a half mile on his hands and knees toward the mare and colt. It's the first time the colt would have ever seen a human before and should be scared, but it's not. The fact that with no rope or halter or feed bucket, my father could stoop up to this colt and begin to rub its legs, back, belly, and head without scaring it is amazing. The key element to this is never allowing your head to be taller than the colt's head.

The Hebrew meaning of the word 'grace' is to stoop or bow. Have you ever realized that the Creator of this world crawls to you for miles (humbly) and comes to you to get to know you? (Remember, he humbled himself.) Listen...God could have walked up to you all proud and tough, but He knew you would run (like the colt) if He did. Remember, He knocks gently at the door to our hearts, He doesn't kick it down (Revelation 3:20). What a unique sight it was to see my dad humble himself to a horse to get to know it, but what an awesome picture it is to see the God who holds each star in place crawl to us in order to save us from eternal death.

GROW! What does grace mean to you? How have you seen God humble himself or stoop in your life? How did you respond? What does grace do to you and for your relationship to Christ?

SHEEPISH ME

READY, *"The Lord is my shepherd, I shall not want." Psalm 23:1*

SET, Whether you've grown up in the Bible belt or not, I bet you've heard or been read the twenty-third Psalm before. You probably never sat and listened intently to the words and asked yourself the question, if the Lord is my shepherd, what does that make me? I'll give you one guess. Time's up...a *sheep!* That's right, a small, smelly, frail little bundle of wool that grazes on pastures. Can you believe that we are called sheep? I mean, come on God, at least give us a little credit and call us something like a lion, Doberman, horse, Brahma bull, or something with a little more clout. Something that doesn't insinuate that we are total wimps, wandering aimlessly, without any brains or brawn to back us up. It's almost like saying, "God, we (the sheep of your flock) are absolutely lost and unprotected without you." *Exactly!*

Let's talk shop about sheep for a minute. Sheep are not real smart, don't have a protective device on them to ward away predators, and can't find food or water without help. Their only defense, and it's weak, against wolves is to run or 'baa-baa' them to death. Basically, the shepherd is the sole existence of a flock of sheep. His job is to protect, provide, and preserve the livelihood of the flock. He is a servant at heart with the sole goal of providing the best and safest environment in which to graze. You and I are no different than the four-legged creatures of the shepherd's flock. We wander out of God's will daily, we need a herdsman to protect us from unwanted assassins of Satan and we can rest assured we are safely watched over by night. Isn't it cool how our God humbles himself daily to provide our every need so that we can put our ol' heads down and just eat away on the pasture of peace, not caring about the wordly wolves that lurk. I don't know about you, but this sheep stuff is not a *baaaaad* deal after all. Baa, baa, baa, baa!

GROW! What kind of sheep are you? Are you an obedient or rebellious type? How can we rest knowing the shepherd watches over us daily? Does that excite you?

159

READY, *"Those who regard vain idols forsake their faithfulness."*
Jonah 2:8

SET, Correct me if I'm wrong, but things just ain't the same as they used to be. Now, I'm not saying that we've reversed in the productivity department, but I am saying we do live in the 'drive thru' mentality. If it's not done quick (less than five minutes), then we don't have time to wait on it. Go to your grandparents' home sometime and talk to them about the way things used to be made....to *last.* Durability, withstanding, and just down right tough were key marketing buzz words in the sales departments. You didn't have to, nor need to, buy a car every three years because at that point you were just getting it broke in real good like a worn pair of jeans. To stick with something like the same job for thirty years and get a gold watch upon retirement is unheard of today. To view a marriage not lasting for a lifetime was frowned upon by the public eye. Not to be loyal to your friend(s) to the core of your heart and not gossip about them behind their backs was as normal as breathing. What has happened to staying power?

Look at the life of our friend in the Bible, Job. Boy, would his life make a great silver screen movie in our time. Riches to rags, plush to poverty, fearless to frailty, happiness to homelessness. Say what you want, but you can't deny the one thing Job did and did well...he *stayed.* He stuck with it through the thick and thin of it. Our world is full of single parent families, prisons full of quitters, and job switching yearly. Understand, as Job did, that staying power means sacrifice and giving up self for others. Jesus exemplified this on the Cross at Calvary to us all. The mentors who roam are loyal, humble, visionary, and not divorced. You, yes, you, have plenty of opportunity to turn back the tables of time to the old ways of thinking and suck it up and stick it out. So do it!

GROW! Do you have a habit of quitting when times get tough? Do you think a pattern of quitting starts small and grows with age? How can you train yourself in staying power?

READY, *"No one puts new wine into old wineskins; otherwise the new wine will burst the skins and it will be spilled out, and the skins will ruin. But new wine must be put into new wineskins and both are preserved." Luke 5:37-38*

SET, Have you ever run across one of those passages of scripture that seemed to have applied to you as much as fleas to a dog? That's right, it just doesn't seem to fit your life, nor does it look like it ever will. For years I seemed to have stumbled over this verse in the gospel of Luke like a big pair of shoes in a dark hallway and never quite clued in to its real meaning. What this verse is saying, simply stated in modern terminology, is to keep the standards, yet apply them and use them more creatively. This whole devotion book is meant to come alive in the present. If you're gonna bore someone, don't bore them with the Bible. It's key that we don't water down the richness of scripture, yet learn new ways and challenge ourselves daily on how we can creatively make God's word more exciting in a stagnant society. You can do things a new, exciting, different way without compromising your commitment to Christ. How about it...take a moment today to sit back and let those creative juices flow. After all, didn't Jesus do this same thing when His life and teachings could not be contained within the old rigid system of the Mosaic Law? Wasn't He the one who first put the new covenant (new wine) into a new generation during His days? Come on hang, let's show this ol' world just how fashionable our faith can really be.

GROW! When was the last time you used a recent event or illustration to prove a point out of past scripture? Try it...it's eye opening!

UNDER DOG

READY, *"Encourage one another day after day as long as it's still called today lest your heart be hardened by the deceitfulness of sin."* Hebrews 3:13

SET, The *Nickelodeon Channel* has a cartoon on each Sunday morning that is a stitch. This goofy little dog in a superman outfit comes out and says, "There's no need to fear, Underdog is here," then flies off to fight crime on the streets. I've personally always been the type to root for the person or team who is supposed to lose. Somebody once asked President Eisenhower why he ever bought that farm of his located in Gettysburg, Pennsylvania. He told them that all of his life he wanted to take a piece of ground which really hadn't been cared for (cultivated or fertilized or watered) and work with everything he had to leave it in better condition than he found it, and that's exactly what he did.

You know, that is such a simple principle, yet it is loaded with truth. Many folks in life, regardless of what they do or where they're from, have that inner urge to make a winner out of a loser. We are always looking for a big challenge, and there is really none too big with God as our source of power and motivation. William Barclay wrote, "One of the highest duties is to encourage others....it is easy to laugh at men's ideals; it is easy to pour cold water on their enthusiasm; it is easy to discourage. The world is full of discouragers. We have a Christian duty to encourage one another. Many a time a word of praise or thanks or appreciation or cheer has kept a man on his feet. Blessed is the man who speaks such a word."

Jesus was the underdog by the world's standards yet became the victor and now sits at the throne of God. With a simple wink of an eye, smile, soft word or serving hand, you can encourage someone to be or do better and follow Christ's example. Don't expect a lot of praise or to sign any autographs for encouraging others because it's definitely not the norm. Don't be one of those folks in life who rains on everyone else's parade...be there with ticker-tape and banners waving high for encouragement.

GROW! Do you ever feel like an underdog? How do you treat the world's underdogs? Are Christians really the underdogs, or ultimate victors?

READY, *"This son of mine was dead and has come to life again; he was lost, and has now been found. And they began to be merry." Luke 15:24*

SET, It's one game we've all played before yet as we get older and graduate from childish games it's still good for some fun watchin.' Ponder with me as we descend upon a game of hide and seek with a bunch of five year olds. The group selects the gullible one of the bunch to be the seeker, as the rest scatter like flies to their secret hideouts. The seeker begins to count to ten (by thousands) then shouts out, "Ready or not, here I come!" Remember how you would always go to the obvious spots first and come up empty handed, so then you would resort to phase two of the search and rescue mission? Finally, after a few minutes, your Sherlock Holmes investigation tactics were successful. The part I never liked about this goofy game (you too, I'll bet) was when you did such a good job of hiding that you never got found. You were the one who wasn't told the game was over, so you stayed in the stinky, dirty, laundry basket camouflaged in socks, underwear and shirts with armpit stains. The object of that game is to eventually be *found*, not remain concealed forever.

Everyone, and I mean everyone, you pass on the streets each day is still, in one form or another, playing hide and seek. The sad thing is that we all really want to be found, because that means we matter. The incredible thing about God is He entered His Son (Jesus) into this game of life to find those who are lost with no hope. No matter how macho, tough, independent, self-reliant a soul may appear to be, it's all a front. In their own way they wiggle and make high-pitch noises and sounds to draw attention from the seeker. As Christians, we need to listen for those noises, gestures, comments, attitudes, and outbursts which are really saying, "I'm over here...come find me." The prodigal son was lost, living in a pig pen and returned to an inaugural ball reception from his father. The same will be true for those lost souls on earth...ready or not, here *He* comes!

GROW! Who do you know that is lost in the game of life from Jesus? Can you help find them?

SEA OF CROWNS

READY, *"And before the throne there was a sea of glass like crystal and in the center and around the throne." Revelation 4:6*

SET, This is one of those verses that has intrigued folks for many moons. Most would pass this right by without catching a glimpse of the true meaning and visualize just what's going on here. Throughout your journey on this Christian road, you, by your efforts in obedience, will be rewarded by our Lord with various crowns. Through your perseverance and endurance in this race you might receive the crown of exultation (1 Thessalonians 2:19), the crown of righteousness (2 Timothy 4:8), the crown of life (James 1:12), or the crown of glory (1 Peter 5:4). All these crowns come after persevering through trials, being approved, who wait for His appearing but all are promised by God to those who truly love Him. In the book of The Revelation, you find contained in John's dream and vision, a sea of believers wearing their crowns, gathered at one place, the foot of the throne, doing one thing. Don't miss this now...they will all be throwing their crowns at the feet of the Savior, praising Him for who He is and what He has done. Wow! A multitude of common folks who have been tested and tried by this wacko world and been found worthy to receive a medal of honor (a crown) to be given back ultimately to the giver.

You, yes you, whether you realize it or not, are accumulating crowns, invisible to ordinary individuals, but seen by the Savior. One day, when we all meet in that place as one body, crowns glistening like a sea of crystals, we will remove them and throw them like Frisbees at the Throne of God. Come on now, partner...if that doesn't jump-start your heart, nothing will. Get excited about an opportunity to be able to give back a small portion to our Lord. Practice up your Frisbee arm because some day it will come in good use.

GROW! Why does God reward us with crowns? What do you think a crown looks like? Are you prepared to give them back to the Creator?

GRADUATION DAY

READY, *"Yet you do not know what your life will be like tomorrow. Your life is but a vapor that appears for a little while and then vanishes away." James 4:14*

SET, Graduation day, whether is be from high school or college is not only an accomplishment, but for some, a relief. The tougher the studies get, the harder the diploma comes. To set out on this adventure is more than taking a course in math or science. To arrive at the final destination in a gym or auditorium dressed in a cap and gown, lookin' like an ordained minister is exciting. To walk down the isle in front of beaming parents and gloating in-laws to receive a certificate of graduation evolves into a memorable moment. Realize it or not, this event is a mirror of real life experiences. It starts in elementary school and ends at death. We all go from the bottle, to crawling, to walking, to talking, to riding a bike, to kindergarten, then elementary school, to junior high, onward to high school, to driving, to college, to career, to marriage, to kiddos who call you mommy or daddy, to retirement, then to the life hereafter. That's the question...what is the hereafter? It will be the ultimate graduation ceremony we all will be a part of. When does it happen? The book of James says like a vapor or mist. The common world can't predict it nor schedule its arrival time.

How do you handle death when it passes by your house? It may come knocking on the door of a parent, coach, friend, or sibling first. It's been said that there are two things we all must do...pay taxes and graduate (die). The purpose of this devo is not to start your day out on a down note, but to get you to thinkin.' Death doesn't have to be sad when you know where you're graduating to. Jesus is the ultimate commencement speaker who holds the certificate of heaven in His, and only His, hands. Do you have family, friends, or others who you know won't be a part of the happy graduation experience? Are you sure that *you* are ready today, at a moment's notice, to walk the isle of eternity with Christ? If yes, then your degree is gonna' take you farther than just a career. If not, maybe you should consider what you're graduating into.

GROW! What scares you most about death? Are you sure you're gonna' receive a diploma of life?

165

HARD WORK

READY, *"God saw all that He had made, and it was very good."*
Genesis 1:31

SET, Growing up in Dallas and working on my father's ranch in Decatur (one hour north of Dallas) presented quite a problem for maintaining sanity at both locations. Consequently, my summers were consumed with building pole barns, welding pipe fence, bucking hay bales, shoeing horses, and brush-hogging three hundred acres of dry Texas coastal grass. Those events translated into what's commonly called 'hard manual labor.' I couldn't believe that my father would ask a budding sixteen year old to sacrifice his summers at pool side for a ten hour day in sweltering one hundred degree heat. Didn't he clue in, or was he born in the dinosaur era, that my main responsibilities were to sleep until noon, eat a tropical lunch by the pool, wax my cool car, and then go to my friend's house to meet new 'chicks' until curfew. Not to say that doing any of that was wrong, lazy, or irresponsible, it just didn't seem to be an option with my dad.

You know, I look back now and seriously do appreciate a huge trait that was passed down to me from my father...a *work ethic.* Don't let me fool you for a minute. I still have a huge lazy streak in me, and I did spend a ton of time just chilling out and cooling out. No matter where you're from, how you've grown up, what your stature is, what your future holds in store for you, or whether you're male or female, hard work is valuable and ordained by our God from the beginning of time. Yes, a key word we can't forget is balance, and few people have found it in our social system. Some are either sluggards, or they are workaholics with no balance whatsoever. The fact is that your work is valued by God and as the Word says is "very good." Work hard when it's time to work, and rest peacefully when it's time to rest. Do me a favor and don't forget to "do all your work heartily for the Lord, not for man." (Colossians 3:23) It makes all your labor not in vain.

GROW! Why is hard work so satisfying? When was the last time you slept soundly because of a hard days work? How can you work hard today?

FENCE WALKERS

READY, *"Where will you be stricken again, as you continue in your rebellion? The whole head is sick and the whole heart is faint." Isaiah 1:5*

SET, Growing up on a ranch all my life sure didn't make me a cowboy or farmer by any stretch of the imagination. One thing it did do is educate me in a few areas that I most likely would have slept through if it were taught in a classroom. One of my father's adventures was in the cattle ranching industry for a 'short' while. I learned a few interesting tid-bits about the nature of a cow. First of all, while buying cows at an auction barn (a real adventure), you can't tell which ones will turn out to be producers, and which ones may be a problem. The first test comes when you first turn out the new cows into the pasture they'll soon call 'home on the range.' One of two things will happen, they'll either adapt to the new living arrangements, or they'll begin to walk the fence line to find a hole and escape captivity. I recall my dad just waiting there the first few hours to see which ones would run through the fence. He would immediately trailer those cows back up and take them to the slaughter house for processing into hamburgers and steaks. Once a fence walker, they'll always be fence walker and they're not worth the trouble of keeping.

Some folks are no different than a cow in that they always look for ways of breaking the barriers (fences) of life, Christian or not. Some folks walk the fences instead of enjoying all the pasture to roam freely in what God's given them. They look for loop-holes in scripture, school, sports, business, family, and commitment. We as Christians can be different. We can live freely and enjoy all that we do have, instead of focusing on the few areas of no-no's we have been warned to stay clear of by God and His Word. Rebellious attitudes and behaviors do nothing but get us in trouble which eventually lead to destruction of our own lives. Don't be a fence walker and be a pasture dweller for God. It's that one loop-hole that will eventually strangle us and send us to the packing plant.

GROW! What areas of your walk with Christ do you try to escape? Why do you do it? What perspective can we have that will allow us to see all the positives of fences (rules) and not focus on the few negatives?

167

READY, "And Elijah answered and said 'If I am a man of God, let fire come down from heaven and consume you and your fifty.' Then the fire of God came down from heaven and consumed him and his fifty."
2 Kings 1:12

SET, Confidence is something to be compared with bravery in a war. Some call it reliance, assurance, certainty, and faith, but scripture calls it faith, trust, hope, conviction, belief, and dependence. My father used to tell me, "If your ability was half of your confidence, you'd be dangerous." The problem we as humans seem to have with confidence is that we have it in the wrong things. We tend to put all our cards on our business brains, athletic attributes, luxurious looks, or witty way with words. This is why so many have such low self-image—because we fail in areas that we rely on self, not God, to be successful.

Elijah, as you probably know, was a great prophet. He was called upon by God to be a communicator and public address system of the truths to come. He was obedient to his calling which allowed him to have divine confidence that his Master's messages would not be mocked and would 'hold water,' so to speak, when tested. Elijah had the confidence (faith) that when he picked up the phone to call upon the Creator, he would not get a busy signal. What trust it must have taken to stand in front of a bunch of doubting dummies and put his God (the Almighty) to the test. It was kinda like a youngster saying, "My dad can beat up your dad." God the Father has not, nor will He ever be made out to be a joke (mocked). Elijah called down the fire from heaven and at once (not a moment's notice) his wish came true in full force. You see, God doesn't do anything half way and this includes showing His power over a false god. Learn from this and know that you worship this same God that shows Himself the all powerful, yet knows how many hairs you have on your head. Have your confidence (faith) in the right thing, not *things.* Remember, they will someday all burn.

GROW! Where does your confidence come? How confident are you in the flesh? Is God the power in your strength?

A Christian's Emancipation Proclamation

READY, *"What shall we say then? Are we to continue to be a slave to sin that grace may increase? May it never be! How shall we who died to sin still be a slave to it?" Romans 6:1-2*

SET, Back in the days of Abraham Lincoln and slavery, we as a nation experienced tremendous tension. Slaves were bought and sold faster than used cars and they had little hope for freedom. That was until Honest Abe came around and released the pressure by signing the Emancipation Proclamation—the slaves' ticket to freedom. His desire was no more chains and poor living conditions, no more beatings and small food portions, no more high fences or free labor, no more long hours and back pain, no more, no more, no more. A weird thing occurred though, when the slaves were told they were free, some stayed with their masters. That's right, some slaves chose to pass on freedom and continue the lifestyle they had known, probably all their long lives.

The apostle Paul writes in the sixth chapter of Romans the emancipation proclamation for Christians who are slaves to the meanest master of all, *sin.* You as a new creature in Christ were a slave bound hopelessly to sin, but through Christ's crucifixion, are now given the bill of rights for freedom. Freedom to look sin in the slithery eyes and say, "get behind me," and walk away from a potential trap. The capability to live, not a perfect life, but a life unshackled by the chains of sin. Jesus sees daily the same problem Lincoln experience—freed slaves returning to their deceitful masters. Choosing to stay under the rule of sin is a choice that could kill. Read through your 'Bill of Freedom' in Romans chapter six until God enlightens you to His truth. Refuse to be contained by a way of life that will take you nowhere but Hell. Why? Because, where there is freedom and hope you'll find happiness and Heaven. Go on...cut those chains of bondage and walk in the love of the Savior to freedom.

GROW! What are you a slave to today? Do you believe you once were captured by sin but now you're free in Christ? Why or why not? How do you cut those chains? Why do some stay slaves even though freedom has been issued?

Where's The Beef?

READY, *"Every word of God is tested; He is a shield to those who take refuge in Him." Proverbs 30:5*

SET, A few years back, the highly visible fast food burger joint named Wendy's had a commercial that to this day echoes a great message. The stage was a second rate burger joint and the actress, an elderly woman of about seventy-five years with a big mouth, big nose, and the voice of a bass singer shouting out the words, "Where's the beef?" She would prance up to the counter with the grace of a football lineman and demand an explanation for a burger with lettuce, tomato, pickles, onions on a big bun, and a puny little patty of meat. Her beef was why all the flash but no real meat to show for it? Why not put the emphasis on the primary content of a *real* burger? This would (hopefully) lead the viewers to come to Wendy's where a burger with *beef* is the way to go.

As you look around in our Christian culture, you find normal people yelping out a request and petition for 'beef.' Folks are looking for real meat in scripture, to answer questions they are asking. They are asking for help in finding the real substance of scripture and not merely the toppings. You might think that most folks wouldn't want to hear the untainted truths of the Bible, but they do. I'm sure you would much rather hear the words of God rather than someone's philosophy or theology. It never fails to hold water that people desire the truth over the theories. Be a part of the solution of this modern day search for the truth, not the problem. Pointing people back to the Word takes the pressure off you and puts it on the inspired word of God which doesn't leak. You can be like Wendy's and provide for the hungry with the real beef of life...the Word!

GROW! When you share with someone, do you give them the beef of the Bible or toppings of theory? Do you believe the Word is the inspired word? Why? Do you use it as such?

READY, "Now faith is the assurance of things hoped for and the conviction of things not yet seen." Hebrews 11:1

SET, Have you ever asked yourself why this race we call Christianity is a marathon and not a sprint? Boy, oh boy, would it be one heck of a lot less tiring and complicated if it was. Just think...it if was a sprint, it would be like a fast food drive-through where we put our order in and in just a matter of seconds, could see the end product. Take a look at some people of the past whom God called to strap on the lightweight running shoes and start runnin.' Noah for instance was called to build a yacht in the middle of a dry spell in preparation for one whopper of a downpour that would last forty days. One hundred and twenty years God commanded those crazy antics it happened...and boy did it happen! For Noah's willingness to run, God spared his life and his family's. Look at Sarah, Abraham's wife who was unable to have kids, and then at the age of ninety became pregnant with Isaac. Imagine what the neighbors said! What about Moses who was called to lead some three million whiny babies out of slavery and pulled off a few smooth moves along the way like parting a sea, making a river turn to blood, and watching his cane become an irate snake?

The reason we are called to this marathon is because you don't need faith or training to run a sprint. You can see the finish in a sprint from the start but you can't on a marathon. You and anyone else can run a sprint any time (it may take a calendar year) and finish, but a marathon takes extensive training and sacrifice. Admit it, you need God's help to finish this long race with the faith that He will have a final finishing place (heaven) to rest. Our reward is eternal, our endurance imperative, and our course unpredictable, yet exciting. So what are you waiting for...on your mark, get set, go!

GROW! What is the toughest part of your race? What causes you to want to quit? How can others before you like Noah, Sarah, and Moses, inspire you today?

Tight Lipped

READY, "*What I tell you in the darkness, speak in the light; and what you hear whispered in your ear, proclaim upon housetops.*"
Matthew 10:27

SET, I'll never forget that first step. It was a dooser of a drop-off too, but well worth the effort. It was my junior year of college and my year to have a shot at being one of five starters for the upcoming season. Our team had just come off a championship season making it to the top ten in the nation. I had worked at a Christian sports camp called Kanakuk, in the Ozark mountains, in southwest Missouri that summer. It had been a great summer of off-season training along with the benefits of being around other division one athletes who had a tough time too of making this Christian stuff work in the 'big time' on and off the court. I had been really challenged to take a stand for Christ (which I knew meant a fall), but it would mean standing alone cuz' I was the only Christian on the team of fifteen, coaches included. I'll never forget my room mate I'd had for two years prior asking me how summer was and where I'd been, the day we all reported to training on August 20, 1980. I knew this was my first test, but I was scared spit-less to share about Jesus to a guy I had been pretty wild with for two years. I knew he'd think I 'got religious or something' if I shared, but I had to, so I did it. I was right...he asked me what I'd been smokin' and why I'd even waste a summer at a camp full of *do-gooder Bible beaters!*

That was the beginning but I can tell you that seeing me take a stand and change my past lifestyle so radically was testimony enough for three players and my head coach to become Christians. I know I was only a part of the process, not the reason, but what an awesome reward from God for a job well done in faith. Just like this verse says, whatever lessons you learn, convictions you acquire, habits you break, or faith you attain, shout it loud from a point where all can hear. Trust me again, the view from the top with God is majestic.

GROW! Does witnessing to others about what Jesus Christ has done for you, scare you? Why do you think that is? What can you do today to begin to be comfortable about sharing your faith? Have you earned the right to be heard by being a good friend?

COMFORT ZONE

READY, "*This is my comfort in my affliction, that thy word has revived me.*" *Psalm 119:50*

SET, Those wonder years in junior high are stepping stones for some, but potholes for most. Between the ages of twelve and fifteen seems to be a sort of testing ground for finding one's self. By that I mean that most young teenagers are kinda' learning the ropes of this world. During those molding years we first realize the importance of being accepted by our peers, styles of clothes, girls instead of G.I. Joe or guys instead of Barbie, and the latest in cool lingo. We're kinda' setting down those roots that will either make or break us when we start off, head first, into high school. It's funny, but in a way it's not, to see how we all react in those situations we get ourselves into, and squirm our way out of. Those are the times that seem to come our way far too often when we are out of our so-called 'comfort zones.' These zones are like climate changes that make it difficult to adapt quickly. They're those times when we try to be casual in a certain situation, but find we fit about as well as a square block in a round hole.

We all, admit it or not, have a zone or shield around us that is booby trapped with alarms, flashing lights, and sirens. Inside this zone we begin to use body language and double talk (babble) to protect us from the intruder. All of us desire to be accepted, not rejected, by society and friends but at times we feel very uncomfortable. Comfort itself is a kind of utopia that we can relax in and feel like we have what it takes to be 'with it' in a certain situation. God definitely has a sense of humor, judging by the way He puts us in circumstances to kinda' humble us and allow us to realize we need Him to be 'hip.' God's Word is a tremendous kick-stand to fall back on every day when we do (and we will) get into those certain situations where we feel we will 'lose face.' When they come, He will be there. Your comfort should always lie in God and if you look at His word there are no rejection zones to deal with. Yippee!

GROW! What sort of circumstances make you feel most uncomfortable? What type of alarm system do you have that is set off by discomfort? How can God's word aid in this struggle? What visual ways do you show you're not feeling like you fit in?

READY, "See, I am doing a new thing! Now it springs up; do you not perceive it? I am making a way in the desert and streams in the wasteland." Isaiah 43:19

SET, It was news that literally stopped the athletic world dead in its tracks. In the late 80's there was a young man who played basketball for the University of Maryland (in the glory years) and got the attention of the sports media. His name, Len Bias. His future, top round draft choice of the Boston Celtics, and a consistent contender each year for the NTSA championship. Len Bias was supposed to rekindle the flame of the fans and world championship flags that hang so proudly from the ceiling of The Boston Garden. Tragic news hit the press when Len died prior to his first season from misuse of the illegal drug cocaine. He hadn't been an avid user, or pusher, or even addicted—just a one-time thing. *Sports Illustrated* interviewed his high school coach who was quoted as saying, "I guess the fast lane got even faster."

We seem to live in a world which spends its time training on the fast track. Too busy to stop along life's journeys and love life. Too hurried to enjoy what few minutes we are allowed to rent the air we breath. Are you sick of thinking that you're working your life to an existence filled with regrets? Perhaps it's time that we check out of the rat race. It's not a winnable race anyway. Get back to the basics of life and that's loving God, loving your family, loving your friends (in that order). This treadmill will take you nowhere fast and it takes your eyes off your Savior too! Pull the plug on this new high tech machine we call life in the fast lane, and begin to abide (which means rest) in a great big God who's ready to just 'chill out' for a minute with *you.*

GROW! Are you tired of going fast and feeling like you've gone nowhere? Are you ready to reside in your Creator's comfort? Start now by letting go and getting off.

COMMITMENT

READY, "And as they were going along the road, someone said to Him, 'I will follow you wherever you go.'" Luke 9:57

SET, What an awesome, bowed-up statement this is. There are very few people who would take a mouthful of commitment like that and say it. The multitudes today would at best only follow at a distance and when the heat was turned up, run for the hills. To Jesus, being committed means a one hundred percent sold out, lock and load, willing to die definition. Our society will jump on the band wagon for a cause like animal rights, gay rights, historical rights, minority rights, but not for Jesus' rights. Webster defines commitment as a pledge or promise to do something for some person, place, or thing. Other religions like Jehovah's Witness, Mormon, Buddhism, Islam, and New Age, are, for the most part more committed to their cause than we are our own. You know, when you get right down to the brass tacks of it, to be committed you have to believe whole-heartedly first.

What are Christians honestly to be committed to? Five things:
1.   Committed to the word of God (2 Timothy 3:17-17)
2.   Committed to God's will, not ours (Ephesians 2:8-10)
3.   Committed to be obedient to the demand of Christian life (2 Timothy 2:4-8)
4.   Committed to the total cost (2 Timothy 1:8)
5.   Committed to making disciples (2 Timothy 2:2)

You won't be an effective follower of Jesus if you become disobedient and take your eyes off Him. The different stages of obedience are: don't care, me first then you, Jesus first then He will surely give back to me, and lastly, true obedience is give no matter what is in store for me. Satisfaction like you've never experienced before will surface after you commit your life totally to your Savior. All these movements we stand for in our culture are great but they can't hold a candle to the cause of Christ. Make a movement for the Master today!

GROW! Define what commitment means to you? What are you most committed to today? What hinders you to becoming totally committed to Christ?

READY, *"Do not be unequally yoked to non-believers; for what partnership have righteousness and lawlessness or what fellowship has light and darkness?" 2 Corinthians 6:14*

"Bad company corrupts good morals." 1 Corinthians 15:33

SET, You know something? Being a Christian and a friend can at times drive you crazy. We, as followers of Jesus, are called to live *in* this stinky world but not be *of* it. We are called to share our biggest joy with non-followers yet not get sucked into the cave of compromise. A friend of mine told me that who and what I hang out with is probably what I will become. Let me put that in English for you, if you hang around the pigs long enough, you'll probably get pretty fond of the mud. The Bible tells us (warns us really) to beware of what type of people we 'yoke' ourselves to. A yoke can best be described as a large wooden harness which goes over the back of a team of oxen's neck to provide steering and stability to the plow. When the yoke is not fitted properly or if two oxen of different sizes or types are put together, they go at a different speed and plow a crooked row. The result is frustration on the farmer's part and extended work hours to redo mistakes. But put a team of oxen of identical size and type together and the outcome is a nicely plowed field in which to plant a crop.

You see, the apostle Paul knew that if we, as Christians, were to yoke ourselves to a non-Christian as a companion our life would be pretty tough to steer. The result is a difference in beliefs, philosophies, actions, morals, ethics and destinations for eternity. No, I'm not saying not to associate yourself with non-Christians each day, just don't yoke yourself to them. Be a light and witness to them but not a fox hole mate. Trust me, your life won't be such an up and down roller coaster ride if you follow Paul's advice...if anyone knew, he surely did.

GROW! Do you yoke yourself to non-Christians? Why? Why should we not? What benefits are there in yoking to a fellow follower?